McGwire

and Sosa

Welcome Rain

THIS IS A WELCOME RAIN BOOK

Copyright © Carlton Books Ltd, 1998

First published in 1998 by Carlton Books Ltd,
20 St Anne's Court, Wardour Street, London W1V 3AW

This edition published in association with
Welcome Rain
532 LaGuardia Place
Box no. 473
New York NY10012

10 9 8 7 6 5 4 3 2 1

First edition 1998

A CIP catalogue record for this book is available from the British Library

ISBN 1 56649 148 7

Printed and bound in Italy

Baseball's Greatest Home Run Story...

GEORGE VECSEY has seen it all. As a child he attended one of Babe Ruth's last appearances in Yankee Stadium. As a young reporter in 1961, he covered approximately 40 of Roger Maris' games and in 1998, he remains one of America's most respected baseball reporters. In a record-breaking season, the *New York Times* sports columnist sets the year in context, providing an insight into the men who set the mark and the men who captured the hearts of all Americans during a spectacular duel which put baseball back on the world's sporting map.

a LL SEASON LONG, Mark McGwire and Sammy Sosa continued to hit home runs. They never let the pressure get to them. They never went into a long slump. They just kept slugging, passing Babe Ruth, passing Roger Maris, pushing each other toward some new level for power and consistency.

But some of the most beautiful events in the Mark McGwire-Sammy Sosa saga did not take place at home plate.

Some of these defining moments took place on the field, when McGwire and Sosa discovered each other as kindred souls, sluggers who understood each other. Sosa may have surprised McGwire by giving him a Latin-style "abrazo"—a hug with a resounding thump on the back—but McGwire showed his respect back many times.

In this season of the home run, the two sluggers showed that athletes do not have to display contempt for each other, do not have to insult or intimidate each other.

There was, for example, the morning of September 7 in St. Louis, before Sosa's Chicago Cubs would play McGwire's Cardinals in a century-old Midwestern rivalry. There was no tension as the two men delivered a 30-minute press conference, sitting side by side in an interview room underneath the stands.

Question:	Sammy said you would hit 70 by the end of the year. How many do you think he will hit?
McGwire:	Wouldn't it be great if we just ended up tied? I think it would be beautiful.
Question:	What number?
McGwire:	70 is a good one. (*Laughter from reporters.*)
Sosa:	I will take it.

In this press conference, they turned to each other and laughed, and occasionally gave each other the high-five.

Later that day, McGwire would tie Roger Maris' record for 61 home runs in one season. The next day, McGwire would break the record, and as the Cardinals celebrated, Sammy Sosa ran in from right field and hugged McGwire again.

"Mark is the man," Sosa told everybody.

They both wanted a record, more than they would admit. When McGwire thumped five on the final weekend, to finish with the predicted 70 homers, Sosa finished with 66 after the Cubs victorious play-off with the Giants. But they had both won, and everybody knew it.

Americans expect too much from athletes. They expect athletes to not only perform superbly on the field, but also to set an example for adults and children, to be "role models". All too often, when athletes talk about being role models, there is the cheesy reek of self-promotion. In this case, they did not talk about setting an example, they just did it.

Sosa, a dark-skinned man who had grown up poor in the Dominican Republic, impressed everybody with his joy, his openness.

McGwire, a white man, the son of a California dentist, had once been tense and private in public. In this year of the home run, he discussed how he had sought counseling for his negative moods, and he smiled and waved to fans not only in his home ballpark, but also in places like New York, Pittsburgh and Florida, where they cheered his home runs.

Everyone understands the home run. It is the defining American sporting act of this century—more than a knockout punch by Joe Louis, more than a dunk by Michael Jordan, more than a touchdown pass by Joe Montana. The ball goes over the fence—often enough to keep the attention of American fans.

Mark McGwire and Sammy Sosa went beyond the physical act of smashing a baseball over the fence. Instinctively, they knew it was good for them, good for the fans—all right, good for business, too—to show that sport does not have to be a rite of rigid self-fulfillment.

"You have to enjoy it," Sosa said in nearly perfect English in September. "It is not going to happen every year, so this is the year that it is happening and we have got to go out there and enjoy it."

By enjoying the moment, by enjoying each other, Mark McGwire and Sammy Sosa thrilled millions.

h ALF A CENTURY AFTER HIS DEATH, Babe Ruth is still Babe Ruth—baseball's singular player. The Babe. The Sultan of Swat. The Bambino. Big swing. Big smile. Big cigar. Big appetite. The primitive images of him running around the bases, his pitty-pat steps even more exaggerated by the ancient films.

Until he came along in 1914, baseball was a game of guile and touch and nerve. The big kid from Baltimore was unencumbered by rules. He swung and propelled the lopsided, loosely-knit baseball over a distant fence.

George Herman came up as a pitcher, so good that he won all three World Series games in which he pitched. However, when the baseballs kept flying over the fence, he was too good to waste on the bench, so they made him a right fielder and he escalated his league-leading home run total from 11 in 1918 to 29 in 1919.

After that season, the Boston Red Sox sold Ruth to the New York Yankees, still the worst transaction in the history of American sports. He responded by helping to save his sport.

In the middle of the 1920 season, the word got out that eight players on the Chicago White Sox had been implicated in a plot to lose the 1919 World Series to Cincinnati. The eight players were banished, but Babe Ruth distracted people by blasting 54 homers in 1920, then raising the record to 59 the next year. In 1927, he broke his own record with 60 homers.

By then, the Roaring Twenties were in full riotous stampede. America was in a mood for a good time, and who better to provide the good time than a rollicking athlete who grinned for the cameras and waved at the fans and was famous for his excesses? And baseball survived and thrived.

14

Don't buy the revisionist legend—spread mostly on talk radio, among youths who do not read—that Ruth was some "fat guy who hit home runs". For a long time, he was a nimble and quick-witted fielder and base-runner, at least until age and weight caught up with him in the 1930s.

It did not end well for the Babe. Nobody ever asked him to manage, and he spent many years at the fringe of the game. He died of cancer in 1948 at the age of 53, but his legend never faded.

When Maris hit 61 homers in 1961, he felt the sneers that he was no Babe Ruth. Henry Aaron, distinguished and skilled, wound up with 755 home runs, and felt the resentments, complicated by the racist element in America that felt a black man should never surpass Babe Ruth.

There were no resentments by 1998. "Babe Ruth, what can you say?" McGwire said on September 5, the day he caught the Babe with 60. "You are almost speechless when people put your name alongside his name. I wish I can go back in time and meet him. Obviously, he was probably the most important sports figure in the world of that time. Hopefully, someday when I pass away, I get to meet him, and then I can really truly find out what he was really like."

In their summer of glory, McGwire and Sosa accepted him as a glorious presence, a myth based on reality. He was the Babe.

f OR BETTER OR WORSE, Roger Maris happened to hit 61 home runs, more than any player had ever hit in one season. Immediately, the baseball establishment hung an asterisk around his neck that seemed to clang as loud as a cowbell—and could still be heard, 37 years later. He came out of Fargo, North Dakota, a northern outpost that produces people of terse honesty, like Roger Maris. Thick-muscled yet quick and supple, he impressed the New York Yankees enough that they traded for him in 1960. Casey Stengel, the garrulous manager, was enthralled by the new man's base-running and fielding abilities.

In his first season with the Yankees, Maris hit 39 homers with a compact, left-handed swing that was perfect for reaching the short porch in right field at Yankee Stadium. He was voted the Most Valuable Player in his league; there were also rumors that Maris resented Mickey Mantle, and vice versa. The truth was that they shared an apartment in New York, and often joked about how the fickle fans had finally adopted Mantle.

In 1961, Maris led Mantle in an assault on Babe Ruth's record. Pursued by growing numbers of the press, he discovered patches of his hair turning gray, almost overnight.

The league had expanded from eight teams to ten, and the schedule had jumped from 154 to 162 games, so Baseball commissioner Ford C. Frick announced that the home run record would be based upon the old schedule.

This decision embittered Maris, who hit his 59th homer in the 154th game, his 60th in the 159th game and his 61st in the final and 162nd game. He ran the bases quickly, almost apologetically, and although his teammates mobbed him in the dugout, there was no gigantic celebration, no fireworks, no calls from the President.

Treated as something of an imposter, Maris became sour in the subsequent years. He hurt his hand, could not grip a bat, and was never the same player again. He finished his career with St. Louis and finished

with 275 home runs and a career batting average of .260; both far below the level of the sluggers in the Baseball Hall of Fame. He died of cancer in 1985, at the age of 54, living only one year more than Babe Ruth had done.

It was not until after Maris' death that baseball officially made his 61 homers the only single-season record in the books.

As McGwire and Sosa enjoyed their marvelous seasons in 1998, baseball paid homage to Roger Maris. His widow and six children were welcome in St. Louis, where McGwire would hit his 60th, 61st and 62nd homers.

"I think back and I really feel for what he went through, for all the negative stuff that was going on in his life," said a respectful Mark McGwire. "I wish it didn't happen."

The Maris family was hoping the attention would persuade the Old-Timers' Committee to vote their father into the Hall of Fame. Maris' teammates noted that he had played in seven World Series—the mark of a winner.

One thing was rarely mentioned in 1998: Roger Maris still held the American League record for home runs in one season—a bittersweet honor for a very good ball player who had one superb season, and never enjoyed it. Ford C. Frick's asterisk had robbed him of his joy.

Mark McGwire

ST. LOUIS CARDINALS

GOING INTO THE 1998 SEASON, Mark McGwire was almost expected to break the home run record of Roger Maris because of the way he had been threatening to do it for a decade. McGwire had the pedigree of a home run champion, although not as early as one might think. When children ask him if he hit a lot of home runs in Little League, he says he was "all right, not great".

He went to one of the most prestigious baseball colleges, the University of Southern California, where his coach, the legendary Rod Dedeaux, tried to use him as a pitcher as well as a hitter. "I just wanted him to keep his options open," Dedeaux said in 1998, proudly attending McGwire's biggest games.

But McGwire knew himself, and insisted on giving up pitching. He turned professional in 1984—and hit exactly one home run in 55 at-bats in his first brief minor league season. Two years later he was playing for the Oakland Athletics, and became a threat to Babe Ruth and Roger Maris almost overnight.

His six-foot, five-inch frame finally adjusted to a powerful home run swing, and in his first full season, 1987, he hit 49 home runs to lead the league. McGwire joined Jose Canseco to become 'The Bash Brothers'—two burly sluggers who congratulated each other with stadium-jarring jolts of their forearms. Nobody got hurt from these monumental collisions, and McGwire had 226 home runs after his sixth full season.

In 1993 and 1994 he was injured, playing in only 74 games, and he began to think about retiring. However, he got his stroke back in 1995, hitting 39 homers in a short season. And then he hit 52 homers in 1996 to lead the league.

In 1997, it was clear that the Oakland franchise could no longer afford him. He hit 34 homers before the Athletics traded him to St. Louis in August, and he hit 24 more homers—giving him 58, and tying the third highest one-season total in history.

At first he thought he was only passing through St. Louis because he wanted to play in southern California near his only child, Matthew. McGwire was divorced, but through an amicable relationship with his former wife and her new husband, he was able to see Matthew regularly.

McGwire changed his plans and signed with the Cardinals because he loved the baseball atmosphere in the old river city. There was a sense of anticipation as he approached 1998. Tony La Russa, his manager, said, "I saw it in his eyes in spring training." McGwire was healthy, and at 35 he was in his prime. Still, nobody could have predicted just how thoroughly he would break the record. On reality, he was the Babe.

Sammy Sosa

CHICAGO CUBS

IN THE YEAR OF THE HOME RUN, Sammy Sosa was the underdog. Few people had thought of him as a man who would go crashing way past the old standards of Babe Ruth and Roger Maris. When he did, baseball fans enjoyed the way he lit up stadiums and television sets with his radiant personality.

Sosa had his own pedigree for baseball: he was born in San Pedro de Macoris in the Dominican Republic, known as the home of major league shortstops. The town also produces a slugger or two.

As a child, Sosa shined shoes to help his mother raise the family. When he was 17, he went to the American minor leagues, and in his fourth season he was brought up to the Texas Rangers.

"He had great talent, he could hit and run and throw," said Bobby Valentine, the manager at the time. "He was a little raw and undisciplined. He would swing at anything, but you could see he was going to be terrific."

The Rangers traded Sosa to the Chicago White Sox, and he played parts of three seasons without inflaming the Windy City. On March 30, 1992, the White Sox traded him to the crosstown Cubs to get an aging outfielder named George Bell.

Playing in the so-called Friendly Confines of Wrigley Field, Sosa listened to coaches who said it was not a crime to watch a pitch go by once in a while. From 1993 through 1997, Sosa hit 170 homers, to give him a total of 207, but his annual totals did not make him a candidate to pass Ruth and Maris.

On May 24, McGwire led him, 24-9, but then Sosa went on a tear, hitting 20 in June alone. By now, American fans were discovering Sammy Sosa. They learned he wore uniform No. 21 as an homage to Roberto Clemente, the great Pittsburgh star from Puerto Rico who had died December 31, 1972, in the crash of a plane he had chartered to carry goods to earthquake-stricken Nicaragua.

"He is a hero to me," Sosa said.

Approaching the age of 30, Sosa became a more selective hitter while the Cubs fought for a wild-card position in the play-offs.

"My situation is different from Mark's," he said. "I'm not looking for home runs. I'm looking for the play-offs." And that's exactly how things ended up.

HOME RUN NO. 1 McGWIRE BECAME THE FIRST PLAYER IN CARDINALS HISTORY TO HIT AN OPENING DAY GRAND SLAM.

Tuesday March 31, 1998

McGWIRE 1	Inning	5	Opponent	Los Angeles Dodgers
	Outs	2	Stadium	Busch Stadium
	Count	1-0	Pitcher	Ramon Martinez
	RBI	4	Distance	364 feet

Thursday April 2, 1998

McGWIRE 2	Inning	12	Opponent	Los Angeles Dodgers
	Outs	2	Stadium	Busch Stadium
	Count	0-1	Pitcher	Frank Lankford
	RBI	3	Distance	368 feet

Friday April 3, 1998

McGWIRE 3	Inning	5	Opponent	San Diego Padres
	Outs	0	Stadium	Busch Stadium
	Count	3-2	Pitcher	Mark Langston
	RBI	2	Distance	364 feet

Saturday April 4, 1998

McGWIRE 4				
	Inning	6	Opponent	San Diego Padres
	Outs	0	Stadium	Busch Stadium
	Count	2-1	Pitcher	Don Wengert
	RBI	3	Distance	419 feet

SOSA 1				
	Inning	3	Opponent	Montreal Expos
	Outs	2	Stadium	Wrigley Field
	Count	2-1	Pitcher	Marc Valdes
	RBI	1	Distance	371 feet

CONGRATULATIONS FROM TEAMMATE TOM LAMPKIN AS McGWIRE CROSSES THE PLATE AFTER HIS OPENING DAY GRAND SLAM AGAINST THE DODGERS.

Saturday April 11, 1998

SOSA 2

Inning	7	Opponent	Montreal Expos
Outs	1	Stadium	Olympic Stadium
Count	1-2	Pitcher	Anthony Telford
RBI	1	Distance	350 feet

Tuesday April 14, 1998

McGWIRE 5

Inning	3	Opponent	Arizona Diamondbacks
Outs	1	Stadium	Busch Stadium
Count	1-2	Pitcher	Jeff Suppan
RBI	2	Distance	424 feet

McGWIRE 6

Inning	5	Opponent	Arizona Diamondbacks
Outs	2	Stadium	Busch Stadium
Count	1-1	Pitcher	Jeff Suppan
RBI	1	Distance	347 feet

McGWIRE 7

Inning	8	Opponent	Arizona Diamondbacks
Outs	0	Stadium	Busch Stadium
Count	2-0	Pitcher	Barry Manuel
RBI	2	Distance	462 feet

> " I'm always amazed by him. I'm not sure if I can come up with any other words to describe him. I'll let you guys who are more creative with words come up with words to describe what a special thing we have here at Busch Stadium."
>
> **CARDINALS MANAGER TONY LA RUSSA**

Wednesday April 15, 1998

SOSA 3

Inning	8	Opponent	New York Mets
Outs	2	Stadium	Shea Stadium
Count	3-2	Pitcher	Dennis Cook
RBI	1	Distance	430 feet

Friday April 17, 1998

McGWIRE 8

Inning	4	Opponent	Philadelphia Phillies
Outs	2	Stadium	Busch Stadium
Count	2-2	Pitcher	Matt Whiteside
RBI	2	Distance	419 feet

THE FIRST OF THREE
HOME RUNS FOR
McGWIRE AGAINST THE
DIAMONDBACKS TO
BREAK AN EIGHT GAME
HOMERLESS DROUGHT.
IT WAS THE THIRD
THREE HOME RUN
GAME OF HIS CAREER
AND HIS FIRST SINCE
JUNE 11, 1995 FOR
OAKLAND AGAINST
BOSTON.

Tuesday April 21, 1998

McGWIRE 9	Inning	3	Opponent	Montreal Expos
	Outs	2	Stadium	Olympic Stadium
	Count	0-0	Pitcher	Trey Moore
	RBI	2	Distance	437 feet

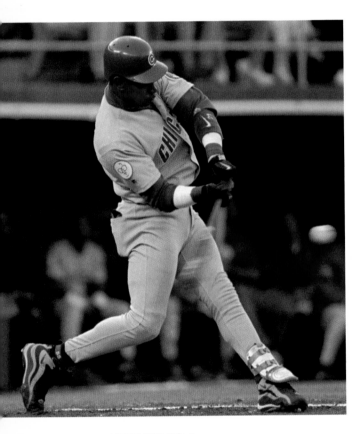

HOME RUN NO. 6
SAMMY SOSA CONNECTS
FOR A TWO RUN HOMER IN
THE FIRST INNING OF THE
CUBS GAME AGAINST THE
PADRES—IN SAN DIEGO.

Thursday April 23, 1998

SOSA 4				
	Inning	9	Opponent	San Diego Padres
	Outs	0	Stadium	Wrigley Field
	Count	0-1	Pitcher	Dan Miceli
	RBI	1	Distance	420 feet

Friday April 24, 1998

SOSA 5				
	Inning	1	Opponent	Los Angeles Dodgers
	Outs	2	Stadium	Dodger Stadium
	Count	3-1	Pitcher	Ismael Valdes
	RBI	1	Distance	430 feet

Saturday April 25, 1998

McGWIRE 10				
	Inning	7	Opponent	Philadelphia Phillies
	Outs	2	Stadium	Veterans Stadium
	Count	1-2	Pitcher	Jerry Spradlin
	RBI	2	Distance	419 feet

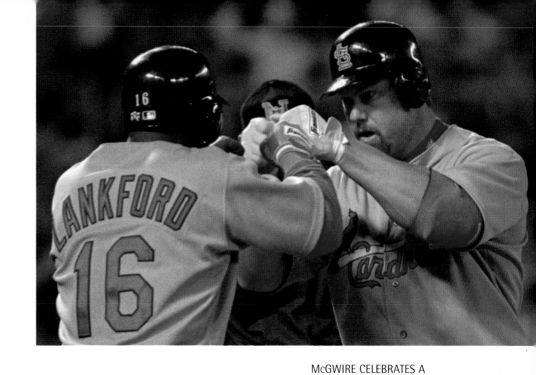

McGWIRE CELEBRATES A TWO RUN SHOT AGAINST THE PHILLIES (HIS TENTH OF THE SEASON) WITH TEAMMATE RAY LANKFORD. HIS TOTAL OF 32 RBIs IN APRIL TIED THE NATIONAL LEAGUE RECORD SET BY BARRY BONDS IN 1996.

Monday April 27, 1998

SOSA 6					
	Inning	1	Opponent	San Diego Padres	
	Outs	1	Stadium	Qualcomm Stadium	
	Count	0-1	Pitcher	Joey Hamilton	
	RBI	2	Distance	434 feet	

Thursday April 30, 1998

McGWIRE 11					
	Inning	8	Opponent	Chicago Cubs	
	Outs	1	Stadium	Wrigley Field	
	Count	2-1	Pitcher	Marc Pisciotta	
	RBI	2	Distance	371 feet	

Friday May 1, 1998

McGWIRE 12					
	Inning	9	Opponent	Chicago Cubs	
	Outs	2	Stadium	Wrigley Field	
	Count	1-2	Pitcher	Rod Beck	
	RBI	2	Distance	362 feet	

Sunday May 3, 1998

SOSA 7					
	Inning	1	Opponent	St. Louis Cardinals	
	Outs	2	Stadium	Wrigley Field	
	Count	2-1	Pitcher	Cliff Politte	
	RBI	1	Distance	370 feet	

BIG MAC CONNECTS FOR THE 400TH CAREER HOME RUN ON MAY 8. HE BECAME THE 26TH PLAYER IN BASEBALL HISTORY TO REACH THAT PLATEAU AND ALSO DID IT IN THE FASTEST TIME IN 4,727 AT-BATS (BEATING BABE RUTH'S 1927 RECORD OF 4,854).

> " I've been the luckiest manager in baseball the last 20 years. And one of the main reasons was because I was able to see Mark McGwire."

CARDINALS MANAGER TONY LA RUSSA

> " When people put my name next to Ruth's name, it still blows me away. I'm still in awe."

MARK McGWIRE

Friday May 8, 1998

McGWIRE 13				
Inning	3	Opponent	New York Mets
Outs	1	Stadium	Shea Stadium
Count	0-2	Pitcher	Rick Reed
RBI	2	Distance	358 feet

McGWIRE WHACKS A TWO RUN HOMER IN THE FOURTH INNING AGAINST THE METS.

McGWIRE WHACKS ONE OVER THE RIGHT FIELD. HIS 15TH HOME RUN OF THE SEASON MEASURED AT 381 FEET.

Tuesday May 12, 1998

McGWIRE 14	Inning	5	Opponent	Milwaukee Brewers
	Outs	0	Stadium	Busch Stadium
	Count	1-2	Pitcher	Paul Wagner
	RBI	3	Distance	527 feet

Thursday May 14, 1998

McGWIRE 15	Inning	4	Opponent	Atlanta Braves
	Outs	0	Stadium	Busch Stadium
	Count	1-1	Pitcher	Kevin Millwood
	RBI	1	Distance	381 feet

"He crushed it. He has the power of three men. I've never faced anybody like him. He's a man among boys."

BREWERS PITCHER PAUL WAGNER

Saturday May 16, 1998

McGWIRE 16	Inning	4	Opponent	Florida Marlins
	Outs	0	Stadium	Busch Stadium
	Count	1-0	Pitcher	Livan Hernandez
	RBI	1	Distance	545 feet

SOSA 8	Inning	3	Opponent	Cincinnati Reds
	Outs	1	Stadium	Cinergy Field
	Count	2-1	Pitcher	Scott Sullivan
	RBI	3	Distance	420 feet

Monday May 18, 1998

McGWIRE 17	Inning	4	Opponent	Florida Marlins
	Outs	0	Stadium	Busch Stadium
	Count	2-0	Pitcher	Jesus Sanchez
	RBI	1	Distance	478 feet

HIGH FIVES ALL AROUND FOR MARK McGWIRE FOLLOWING HIS FOURTH INNING SOLO HOME RUN AGAINST THE FLORIDA MARLINS—HIS 17TH OF THE SEASON.

19, 20

" It's not easy ... I study pitchers. I visualize pitches. That gives me a better chance every time I step into the box.

That doesn't mean I'm going to get a hit every game, but that's one of the reasons I've come a long way as a hitter."

MARK McGWIRE

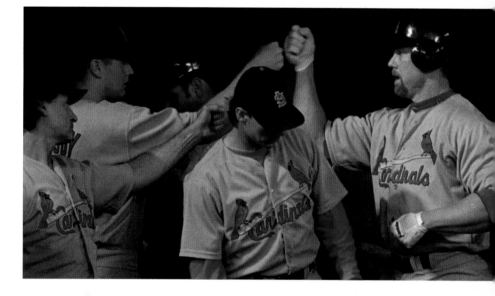

MAC'S THE MAN FOR THE CARDINALS AFTER THE FIRST OF HIS THREE TWO RUN HOMERS AGAINST THE PHILLIES. THE CARDINALS WON THE GAME 10–8.

Tuesday May 19, 1998

McGWIRE 18	Inning	3	Opponent	Philadelphia Phillies
	Outs	1	Stadium	Veterans Stadium
	Count	2-0	Pitcher	Tyler Green
	RBI	2	Distance	440 feet

McGWIRE 19	Inning	5	Opponent	Philadelphia Phillies
	Outs	0	Stadium	Veterans Stadium
	Count	0-2	Pitcher	Tyler Green
	RBI	2	Distance	471 feet

McGWIRE 20	Inning	8	Opponent	Philadelphia Phillies
	Outs	0	Stadium	Veterans Stadium
	Count	0-0	Pitcher	Wayne Gomes
	RBI	2	Distance	451 feet

> **"** McGwire hits the ball further than anyone I've ever seen."

SAN FRANCISCO MANAGER DUSTY BAKER

Friday May 22, 1998

McGWIRE 21

Inning	6	Opponent	San Francisco Giants
Outs	1	Stadium	Busch Stadium
Count	1-1	Pitcher	Mark Gardner
RBI	2	Distance	425 feet

SOSA 9

Inning	1	Opponent	Atlanta Braves
Outs	2	Stadium	Turner Field
Count	2-2	Pitcher	Greg Maddux
RBI	1	Distance	440 feet

Saturday May 23, 1998

McGWIRE 22

Inning	4	Opponent	San Francisco Giants
Outs	1	Stadium	Busch Stadium
Count	1-0	Pitcher	Rich Rodriguez
RBI	1	Distance	366 feet

McGWIRE 23

Inning	5	Opponent	San Francisco Giants
Outs	1	Stadium	Busch Stadium
Count	2-2	Pitcher	John Johnstone
RBI	3	Distance	477 feet

Sunday May 24, 1998

McGWIRE 24

Inning	12	Opponent	San Francisco Giants
Outs	2	Stadium	Busch Stadium
Count	2-2	Pitcher	Robb Nen
RBI	2	Distance	397 feet

TEAMMATES AND MARK McGWIRE DOING THE BONE
AFTER HE SLAMS HIS 25TH HOMER BREAKING THE MAJOR
LEAGUE RECORD FOR HOME RUNS HIT BEFORE JUNE 1.

Monday May 25, 1998

McGWIRE 25					
	Inning	1	Opponent	Colorado Rockies
	Outs	2	Stadium	Busch Stadium
	Count	2-2	Pitcher	John Thomson
	RBI	1	Distance	433 feet

SOSA 10					
	Inning	4	Opponent	Atlanta Braves
	Outs	0	Stadium	Turner Field
	Count	2-2	Pitcher	Kevin Millwood
	RBI	1	Distance	410 feet

SOSA 11					
	Inning	8	Opponent	Atlanta Braves
	Outs	2	Stadium	Turner Field
	Count	0-1	Pitcher	Mike Cather
	RBI	3	Distance	420 feet

SAMMY SOSA AND
FLORIDA MARLINS
CATCHER GREGG ZUAN
WATCH THE FLIGHT OF
HOME RUN NO. 14.
OVER FOUR GAMES
SOSA WENT 8 FOR 17
WITH SIX HOME RUNS
AND 13 RBIs.

Wednesday May 27, 1998

SOSA 12	Inning	8	Opponent	Philadelphia Phillies
	Outs	0	Stadium	Wrigley Field
	Count	1-2	Pitcher	Darrin Winston
	RBI	1	Distance	460 feet

SOSA 13	Inning	9	Opponent	Philadelphia Phillies
	Outs	2	Stadium	Wrigley Field
	Count	0-0	Pitcher	Wayne Gomes
	RBI	2	Distance	400 feet

Friday May 29, 1998

McGWIRE 26	Inning	9	Opponent	San Diego Padres
	Outs	1	Stadium	Qualcomm Stadium
	Count	0-1	Pitcher	Dan Miceli
	RBI	2	Distance	388 feet

McGWIRE SLAMS A NINTH INNING TWO RUN HOMER FOR HIS 26TH OF THE SEASON—HIS 15TH IN MAY—DURING THE CARDINALS 8-3 VICTORY OVER THE SAN DIEGO PADRES.

Saturday May 30, 1998

McGWIRE 27	Inning	1	Opponent	San Diego Padres
	Outs	2	Stadium	Qualcomm Stadium
	Count	0-1	Pitcher	Andy Ashby
	RBI	1	Distance	423 feet

Monday June 1, 1998

SOSA 14	Inning	1	Opponent	Florida Marlins
	Outs	1	Stadium	Wrigley Field
	Count	1-0	Pitcher	Ryan Dempster
	RBI	2	Distance	430 feet

SOSA 15	Inning	8	Opponent	Florida Marlins
	Outs	2	Stadium	Wrigley Field
	Count	1-0	Pitcher	Oscar Henriquez
	RBI	3	Distance	410 feet

" He's not missing mistakes. That's the big thing for all good hitters—McGwire, Griffey and those guys.

They don't swing at bad balls, and they hammer mistakes. They make you pay for every mistake. That's what Sammy's doing."

PHILADELPHIA CATCHER MARK PARENT

SAMMY SOSA TAKES A CURTAIN CALL AFTER HITTING HIS 10TH HOME RUN IN THE
LAST NINE GAMES IN THE CUBS FACE OFF WITH THE WHITE SOX.

Wednesday June 3, 1998

SOSA 16	Inning	5	Opponent	Florida Marlins
	Outs	0	Stadium	Wrigley Field
	Count	1-0	Pitcher	Livan Hernandez
	RBI	2	Distance	370 feet

Friday June 5, 1998

McGWIRE 28	Inning	1	Opponent	San Francisco Giants
	Outs	1	Stadium	Busch Stadium
	Count	1-2	Pitcher	Orel Hershiser
	RBI	2	Distance	409 feet

SOSA 17	Inning	5	Opponent	Chicago White Sox
	Outs	0	Stadium	Wrigley Field
	Count	1-2	Pitcher	Jim Parque
	RBI	2	Distance	370 feet

" We've been riding Sammy the whole time and Sammy's just been terrific."

CUBS MARK GRACE

Saturday June 6, 1998

SOSA 18		
Inning	**7**	*Opponent*	**Chicago White Sox**
Outs	**2**	*Stadium*	**Wrigley Field**
Count	**2-2**	*Pitcher*	**Carlos Castillo**
RBI	**1**	*Distance*	**410 feet**

Sunday June 7, 1998

SOSA 19		
Inning	**5**	*Opponent*	**Chicago White Sox**
Outs	**1**	*Stadium*	**Wrigley Field**
Count	**3-2**	*Pitcher*	**James Baldwin**
RBI	**3**	*Distance*	**380 feet**

Monday June 8, 1998

McGWIRE 29		
Inning	**4**	*Opponent*	**Chicago White Sox**
Outs	**0**	*Stadium*	**Comiskey Park**
Count	**0-0**	*Pitcher*	**Jason Bere**
RBI	**2**	*Distance*	**356 feet**

SOSA 20		
Inning	**3**	*Opponent*	**Minnesota Twins**
Outs	**1**	*Stadium*	**Metrodome**
Count	**0-2**	*Pitcher*	**LaTroy Hawkins**
RBI	**1**	*Distance*	**340 feet**

SOSA ROUNDS THE BASES AS HE RECORDS HOMER NO. 20. HIS 11 HOMERS IN NINE GAMES TIED HACK WILSON AND RYNE SANDBERG FOR THE CUBS CONSECUTIVE GAME HOME RUN RECORD.

❝ I didn't even realize it was a grand slam because I was mentally preparing myself for Andy (Benes) because he struck me out the first time."

MARK McGWIRE

JUNE 12 McGWIRE CLOCKS UP HIS 11TH CAREER GRAND SLAM, HIS SECOND OF THE YEAR. HE HAS HAD AT LEAST ONE HOMER IN THE LAST 11 SERIES TO MOVE INTO THE MAJOR LEAGUE LEAD IN RBIs.

Wednesday June 10, 1998

McGWIRE 30	Inning	3	Opponent	Chicago White Sox
	Outs	1	Stadium	Comiskey Park
	Count	1-0	Pitcher	Jim Parque
	RBI	3	Distance	409 feet

Friday June 12, 1998

McGWIRE 31	Inning	3	Opponent	Arizona Diamondbacks
	Outs	1	Stadium	Bank One Ballpark
	Count	1-0	Pitcher	Andy Benes
	RBI	4	Distance	438 feet

Saturday June 13, 1998

SOSA 21	Inning	6	Opponent	Philadelphia Phillies
	Outs	0	Stadium	Veterans Stadium
	Count	0-1	Pitcher	Mark Portugal
	RBI	2	Distance	350 feet

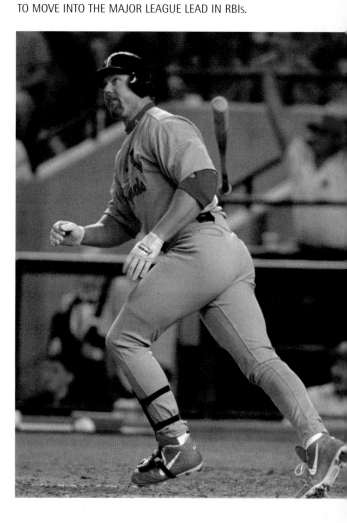

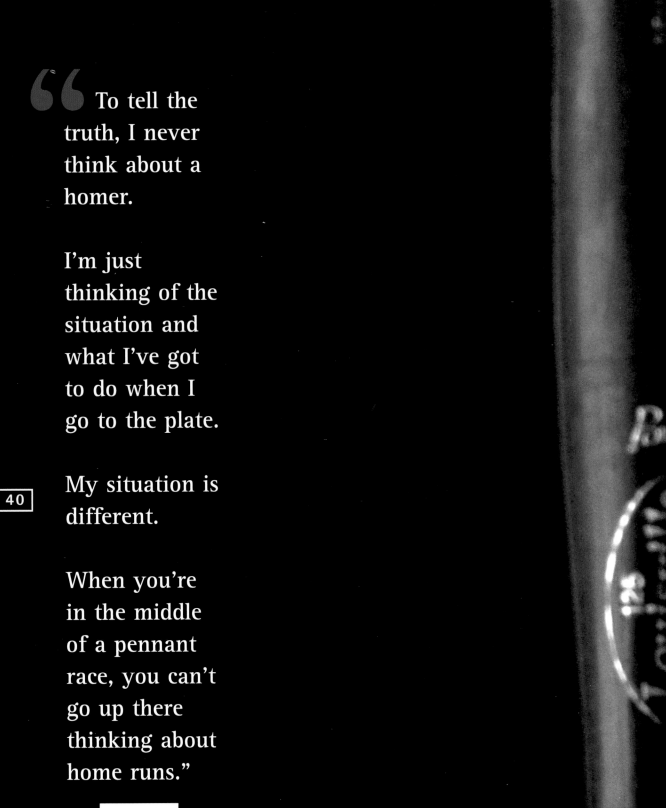

" To tell the truth, I never think about a homer.

I'm just thinking of the situation and what I've got to do when I go to the plate.

My situation is different.

When you're in the middle of a pennant race, you can't go up there thinking about home runs."

SAMMY SOSA

SOSA'S SEVENTH INNING
HOME RUN WAS HIS THIRD
OF THE NIGHT AGAINST THE
MILWAUKEE BREWERS.

Monday June 15, 1998

SOSA 22	Inning	1	Opponent	Milwaukee Brewers
	Outs	2	Stadium	Wrigley Field
	Count	1-0	Pitcher	Cal Eldred
	RBI	1	Distance	420 feet

SOSA 23	Inning	3	Opponent	Milwaukee Brewers
	Outs	1	Stadium	Wrigley Field
	Count	2-1	Pitcher	Cal Eldred
	RBI	1	Distance	410 feet

SOSA 24	Inning	7	Opponent	Milwaukee Brewers
	Outs	2	Stadium	Wrigley Field
	Count	2-1	Pitcher	Cal Eldred
	RBI	1	Distance	415 feet

"I'm seeing the ball well. I'm not trying for home runs. I'm trying to hit to right field more. When I do that, the home runs come."

SAMMY SOSA

Wednesday June 17, 1998

McGWIRE 32	Inning	3	Opponent	Houston Astros
	Outs	2	Stadium	The Astrodome
	Count	1-2	Pitcher	Jose Lima
	RBI	1	Distance	347 feet

SOSA 25	Inning	4	Opponent	Milwaukee Brewers
	Outs	0	Stadium	Wrigley Field
	Count	2-2	Pitcher	Bronswell Patrick
	RBI	1	Distance	430 feet

Thursday June 18, 1998

McGWIRE 33	Inning	5	Opponent	Houston Astros
	Outs	0	Stadium	The Astrodome
	Count	1-1	Pitcher	Shane Reynolds
	RBI	1	Distance	449 feet

Friday June 19, 1998

SOSA 26					
	Inning	1	*Opponent*		**Philadelphia Phillies**
	Outs	2	*Stadium*		**Wrigley Field**
	Count	2-2	*Pitcher*		**Carlton Loewer**
	RBI	1	*Distance*		**380 feet**

SOSA 27					
	Inning	5	*Opponent*		**Philadelphia Phillies**
	Outs	1	*Stadium*		**Wrigley Field**
	Count	1-0	*Pitcher*		**Carlton Loewer**
	RBI	2	*Distance*		**380 feet**

44

"Don't compare me to Babe Ruth.

God gave me the opportunity and the ability to be here at the right time at the right moment, just like He gave Babe Ruth when he was playing.

I just hope I can keep doing what I've been doing, keep taking care of business."

SAMMY SOSA

Saturday June 20, 1998

SOSA 28	Inning	3	Opponent	Philadelphia Phillies
	Outs	2	Stadium	Wrigley Field
	Count	3-2	Pitcher	Matt Beech
	RBI	2	Distance	366 feet

SOSA 29	Inning	6	Opponent	Philadelphia Phillies
	Outs	1	Stadium	Wrigley Field
	Count	2-0	Pitcher	Toby Borland
	RBI	3	Distance	500 feet

SOSA CAME OUT SWINGING FOR THE FENCES AND MISSED, BUT LATER THAT NIGHT HE STRUCK WITH NOS. 28 AND 29.

Sunday June 21, 1998

SOSA 30	Inning	4	Opponent	Philadelphia Phillies
	Outs	2	Stadium	Wrigley Field
	Count	2-2	Pitcher	Tyler Green
	RBI	1	Distance	380 feet

" Right now what's in my mind is going up there and being disciplined.

I was swinging at so many pitches out of the strike zone, and when you do that, you're not going to get a chance to hit strikes. It makes it easier for the pitcher every time I do that."

SAMMY SOSA

SOSA ROUNDS THE BASES FOR HOME RUN NO. 31 TO TIE THE ALL TIME RECORD FOR THE NUMBER OF HOMERS IN A MONTH—18—IN THE CUBS VISIT TO DETROIT.

Wednesday June 24, 1998

McGWIRE 34				
Inning	4	Opponent	Cleveland Indians
Outs	1	Stadium	Jacobs Field
Count	1-1	Pitcher	Jaret Wright
RBI	1	Distance	433 feet

SOSA 31				
Inning	1	Opponent	Detroit Tigers
Outs	1	Stadium	Tiger Stadium
Count	0-2	Pitcher	Seth Greisinger
RBI	1	Distance	390 feet

> **"** I'm real happy my name is in the record book, but it means nothing because we lost."

A HOME RUN IN THE SEVENTH AGAINST THE DETROIT TIGERS GAVE SOSA 19 IN THE MONTH TO BREAK THE MAJOR LEAGUE RECORD AND TOOK HIS SEASON'S TOTAL TO 32.

Thursday June 25, 1998

McGWIRE 35	Inning	1	Opponent	Cleveland Indians
	Outs	2	Stadium	Jacobs Field
	Count	2-2	Pitcher	Dave Burba
	RBI	1	Distance	461 feet

SOSA 32	Inning	7	Opponent	Detroit Tigers
	Outs	0	Stadium	Tiger Stadium
	Count	1-0	Pitcher	Brian Moehler
	RBI	1	Distance	400 feet

Saturday June 27, 1998

McGWIRE 36	Inning	7	Opponent	Minnesota Twins
	Outs	2	Stadium	Metrodome
	Count	2-2	Pitcher	Mike Trombley
	RBI	2	Distance	431 feet

SAMMY SWATS HIS 20TH HOMER OF JUNE IN THE GAME AGAINST THE DIAMONDBACKS
TO COMPLETE A REMARKABLE MONTH AND TO TAKE HIS SEASON TOTAL TO 33.

Tuesday June 30, 1998

> " I would like to
> have another month
> like that. It was a
> pretty good month."

SAMMY SOSA

48

McGWIRE 37	Inning	7	Opponent	Kansas City Royals
	Outs	0	Stadium	Busch Stadium
	Count	0-1	Pitcher	Glendon Rusch
	RBI	1	Distance	472 feet

SOSA 33	Inning	8	Opponent	Arizona Diamondbacks
	Outs	1	Stadium	Wrigley Field
	Count	3-2	Pitcher	Alan Embree
	RBI	1	Distance	364 feet

WITH NO. 37, MARK
McGWIRE, THE NEW
SULTAN OF SWAT, TIED
REGGIE JACKSON'S
RECORD FOR THE MOST
HOMERS BEFORE THE
ALL-STAR BREAK.

Thursday July 9, 1998

SOSA 34			
Inning	2	Opponent	Milwaukee Brewers
Outs	2	Stadium	County Stadium
Count	0-2	Pitcher	Jeff Juden
RBI	2	Distance	432 feet

Friday July 10, 1998

SOSA 35			
Inning	2	Opponent	Milwaukee Brewers
Outs	0	Stadium	County Stadium
Count	1-0	Pitcher	Scott Karl
RBI	1	Distance	428 feet

SOSA SMASHES HOMER NO. 35 IN THE SECOND INNING AGAINST THE BREWERS AT MILWAUKEE.

A 485-FOOT HOMER FOR McGWIRE IN THE IITH INNING GAVE THE CARDINALS A 4–3 VICTORY OVER THE ASTROS.

51

Saturday July 11, 1998

McGWIRE 38			
Inning	11	Opponent	Houston Astros
Outs	1	Stadium	Busch Stadium
Count	0-2	Pitcher	Billy Wagner
RBI	2	Distance	485 feet

> " When he hits line drives, get the family of four out of the left-field seats before they get killed. Without a doubt, this is his year."

BIG MAC TOYS WITH
TEN-YEAR-OLD SON
MATTHEW AFTER HIS
38TH HOME RUN
OF THE SEASON.

> " Mark McGwire's arms are bigger than my legs."

" I've not been around too long, but the home run he hit off me was the most impressive thing I've seen in my major league career."

HOUSTON ROOKIE SCOTT ELARTON

Sunday July 12, 1998

McGWIRE **39**				
	Inning	1	*Opponent*	Houston Astros
	Outs	2	*Stadium*	Busch Stadium
	Count	0-0	*Pitcher*	Sean Bergman
	RBI	1	*Distance*	405 feet

McGWIRE **40**				
	Inning	7	*Opponent*	Houston Astros
	Outs	0	*Stadium*	Busch Stadium
	Count	2-1	*Pitcher*	Scott Elarton
	RBI	1	*Distance*	415 feet

McGWIRE HITS HOME RUNS NOS. 39 AND 40 TO BREAK TWO RECORDS FOR HITTING 40 HOMERS THIS EARLY IN THE SEASON. HE BEAT HIS OWN RECORD FOR GETTING THERE IN THE FEWEST AT-BATS (281 BREAKING HIS 1996 TOTAL OF 294), AND DID SO IN THE CARDINALS 40TH GAME OF THE SEASON— BETTERING BABE RUTH'S 1928 MARK BY ONE GAME.

Some of the longest home runs I've hit, I didn't actually realize they were going that far.

Everyone says, 'What does it feel like to hit the ball that far?'

Actually, there's no feeling at all. I know when the ball meets the bat whether or not it's left the park. It's a nice easy thing."

MARK McGWIRE

McGWIRE CONNECTS FOR HIS 42ND HOMER OF THE YEAR IN THE EIGHTH INNING AGAINST THE LOS ANGELES DODGERS. IT WAS McGWIRE'S SECOND HOME RUN OF THE GAME AND SET A MAJOR LEAGUE RECORD FOR THE MOST HOME RUNS BY THE END OF JULY, SURPASSING BABE RUTH AND JIMMIE FOXX BY ONE HOMER.

Friday July 17, 1998

McGWIRE 41				
	Inning	1	Opponent	Los Angeles Dodgers
	Outs	2	Stadium	Busch Stadium
	Count	0-0	Pitcher	Brian Bohanon
	RBI	1	Distance	511 feet

McGWIRE 42				
	Inning	8	Opponent	Los Angeles Dodgers
	Outs	1	Stadium	Busch Stadium
	Count	1-0	Pitcher	Antonio Osuna
	RBI	1	Distance	425 feet

SOSA 36				
	Inning	6	Opponent	Florida Marlins
	Outs	2	Stadium	Pro Player Stadium
	Count	2-1	Pitcher	Kirt Ojala
	RBI	2	Distance	440 feet

"Mark is just a good hitter, with a good eye and a nice short swing.

He also just happens to be the biggest guy on the planet. He hits towering blasts.

You'll be sitting there saying, 'Aw, he didn't quite get that one.' Then it ends up 30 rows in the stands."

CAL RIPKEN JR.

59

A FAMILY AFFAIR.
WAITING TO BAT WITH
SON MATTHEW.

Monday July 20, 1998

McGWIRE 43	Inning	5	Opponent	San Diego Padres
	Outs	0	Stadium	Qualcomm Stadium
	Count	2-1	Pitcher	Brian Boehringer
	RBI	2	Distance	458 feet

Wednesday July 22, 1998

SOSA 37	Inning	8	Opponent	Montreal Expos
	Outs	2	Stadium	Wrigley Field
	Count	1-0	Pitcher	Miguel Batista
	RBI	3	Distance	365 feet

Sunday July 26, 1998

McGWIRE 44	Inning	4	Opponent	Colorado Rockies
	Outs	2	Stadium	Coors Field
	Count	0-0	Pitcher	John Thomson
	RBI	1	Distance	452 feet

SOSA 38	Inning	6	Opponent	New York Mets
	Outs	1	Stadium	Wrigley Field
	Count	2-2	Pitcher	Rick Reed
	RBI	2	Distance	420 feet

Monday July 27, 1998

SOSA 39	Inning	6	Opponent	Arizona Diamondbacks
	Outs	2	Stadium	Bank One Ballpark
	Count	1-1	Pitcher	Willie Blair
	RBI	2	Distance	350 feet

SOSA 40	Inning	8	Opponent	Arizona Diamondbacks
	Outs	0	Stadium	Bank One Ballpark
	Count	0-0	Pitcher	Alan Embree
	RBI	4	Distance	420 feet

" The thing I sort of get tired of hearing is if I don't hit home runs or don't get hits, that the pressure of the media is getting to me.

Absolutely not.

Believe me, it's not getting to me."

MARK McGWIRE

CUBS THIRD BASE
COACH TOM GAMBOA
CONGRATULATES SOSA
AS HE ROUNDS THE
BASES FOLLOWING HIS
FIRST CAREER GRAND
SLAM—HIS 40TH HOME
RUN OF THE SEASON
AND HIS SECOND OF
THE GAME.

" Sammy has good years every year. This is just an extraordinary year."

CUBS MANAGER JIM RIGGLEMAN

"He's beyond description. I don't know the right words to describe how great a season he's had. You say MVP-type season, but I don't know if that's enough to describe it."

MARK GRACE

45

Tuesday July 28, 1998

McGWIRE 45				
	Inning	8	*Opponent*	Milwaukee Brewers
	Outs	1	*Stadium*	Busch Stadium
	Count	2-2	*Pitcher*	Mike Myers
	RBI	1	*Distance*	408 feet

SOSA 41				
	Inning	5	*Opponent*	Arizona Diamondbacks
	Outs	1	*Stadium*	Bank One Ballpark
	Count	3-1	*Pitcher*	Bob Wolcott
	RBI	4	*Distance*	400 feet

SAMMY WATCHES THE BALL FLY OVER THE FENCE FOR HIS 43RD HOMER OF THE SEASON. IT
WAS AN INTENSE WEEK FOR SOSA AS HE CLOSED THE GAP WITH McGWIRE.

Friday July 31, 1998

SOSA 42				
	Inning	1	*Opponent*	**Colorado Rockies**
	Outs	2	*Stadium*	**Wrigley Field**
	Count	3-2	*Pitcher*	**Jamey Wright**
	RBI	1	*Distance*	**380 feet**

Wednesday August 5, 1998

SOSA 43				
	Inning	3	*Opponent*	**Arizona Diamondbacks**
	Outs	2	*Stadium*	**Wrigley Field**
	Count	3-2	*Pitcher*	**Andy Benes**
	RBI	2	*Distance*	**380 feet**

Saturday August 8, 1998

McGWIRE 46				
	Inning	4	*Opponent*	**Chicago Cubs**
	Outs	0	*Stadium*	**Busch Stadium**
	Count	2-1	*Pitcher*	**Mark Clark**
	RBI	1	*Distance*	**374 feet**

SOSA 44				
	Inning	9	*Opponent*	**St. Louis Cardinals**
	Outs	0	*Stadium*	**Busch Stadium**
	Count	1-0	*Pitcher*	**Rich Croushore**
	RBI	2	*Distance*	**400 feet**

" It's the most excitement we've had in baseball in a long time. The two guys going against each other and the entire country is interested."

OZZIE SMITH, EX–CARDINALS

> "Mark McGwire is 34 years old. I'm 29. He's probably a little bit tired. I'm just having some fun."

SAMMY SOSA

Monday August 10, 1998

SOSA 45				
Inning	5	*Opponent*	San Francisco Giants
Outs	2	*Stadium*	3Com Park
Count	3-1	*Pitcher*	Russ Ortiz
RBI	1	*Distance*	370 feet

SOSA 46				
Inning	7	*Opponent*	San Francisco Giants
Outs	2	*Stadium*	3Com Park
Count	2-1	*Pitcher*	Chris Brock
RBI	1	*Distance*	480 feet

Tuesday August 11, 1998

McGWIRE 47				
Inning	4	*Opponent*	New York Mets
Outs	0	*Stadium*	Busch Stadium
Count	1-0	*Pitcher*	Bobby Jones
RBI	1	*Distance*	464 feet

Sunday August 16, 1998

SOSA 47				
Inning	4	*Opponent*	Houston Astros
Outs	1	*Stadium*	The Astrodome
Count	0-1	*Pitcher*	Sean Bergman
RBI	1	*Distance*	360 feet

> "He consistently hits the ball 475, 500 feet, and if he catches one, who knows, 600 feet. It's ridiculous."

ST. LOUIS BATTING COACH DAVE PARKER

HOMER NO. 47 FOR McGWIRE IN THE GAME AGAINST THE NEW YORK METS. THE BLAST TOOK BIG MAC PAST HACK WILSON'S 1930 NATIONAL LEAGUE RECORD FOR MOST HOME RUNS BY SEPTEMBER 1.

" It's incredible to be able to do what Sammy and Mark are doing. They are kind of feeding off each other ... I've got to root for Sammy. When he hits home runs, we're going to win."

CUBS GARY GAETTI

HEAD TO HEAD
MARK McGWIRE BLOWS A TRADEMARK SAMMY SOSA KISS TO HIS CHICAGO RIVAL AFTER SOSA WALKED IN THE SEVENTH INNING IN ST. LOUIS, AUGUST 19.

THE CROWD GOES WILD AS SOSA PUNCHES UP HOMER NO. 48 AS THE CUBS CLASH WITH
THE CARDINALS, AND TAKES THE LEAD IN THE SINGLE SEASON HOME RUN RECORD FOR THE FIRST TIME—A MARK
THAT LASTED FOR JUST 58 MINUTES.

Wednesday August 19, 1998

McGWIRE 48

Inning	8	Opponent	Chicago Cubs
Outs	1	Stadium	Wrigley Field
Count	3-1	Pitcher	Matt Karchner
RBI	1	Distance	430 feet

McGWIRE 49

Inning	10	Opponent	Chicago Cubs
Outs	1	Stadium	Wrigley Field
Count	2-0	Pitcher	Terry Mulholland
RBI	1	Distance	402 feet

SOSA 48

Inning	5	Opponent	St. Louis Cardinals
Outs	2	Stadium	Wrigley Field
Count	0-0	Pitcher	Kent Bottenfield
RBI	2	Distance	368 feet

" That's why he's the man. That's why I keep telling you that Mark McGwire is the man."

SAMMY SOSA

" It's a privilege to be able to watch these two classy guys go at it like that."

CARDINALS MANAGER TONY LA RUSSA

McGWIRE DRAWS LEVEL WITH HOME RUN NO. 48. NO. 49 CAME IN THE 10TH INNING AFTER SOSA HAD TAKEN THE LEAD IN THE HOME RUN CHASE EARLIER IN THE GAME. "APPARENTLY THE BIG FELLOW TOOK IT PERSONALLY," SAID CARDINALS CATCHER TOM LAMPKIN.

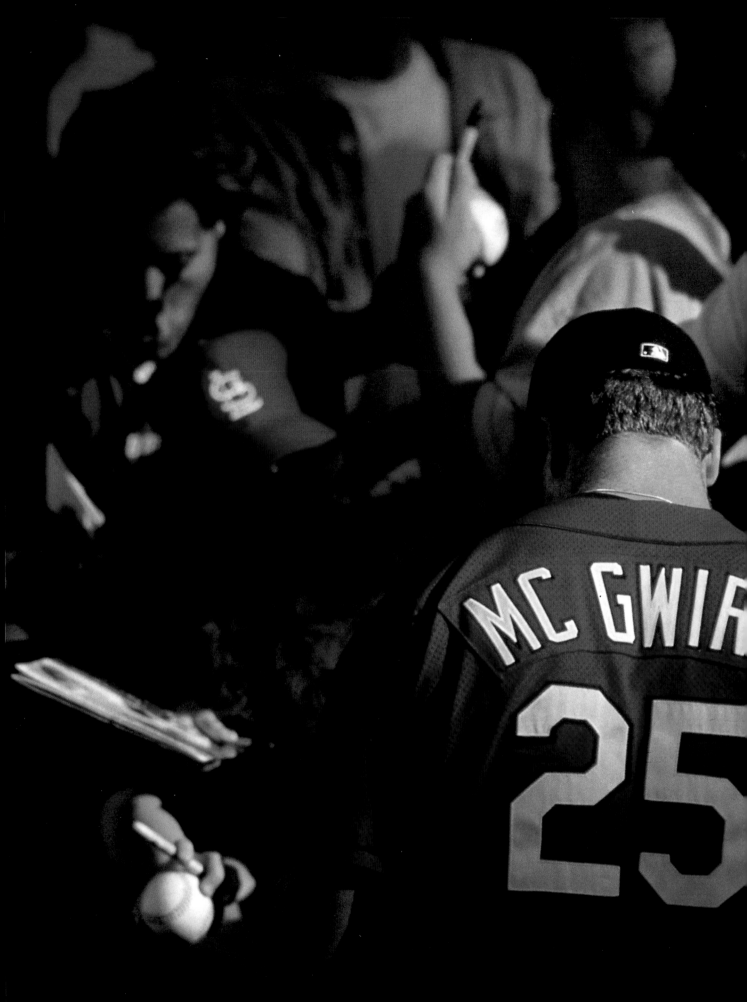

" I wish that
every player
could feel what
I've felt in
visiting ball
parks.

The receptions
I've received…
It's blown
me away.

It's absolutely
remarkable."

MARK McGWIRE

> **"**Only 16 players have hit
> 50 or more homers in a season.
> To me that's a very special
> milestone."

MARK McGWIRE

McGWIRE WATCHES NO. 50 CLEAR THE FENCE IN SHEA STADIUM. HE BECAME THE FIRST
PLAYER IN BASEBALL HISTORY TO HIT 50 HOME RUNS THREE CONSECUTIVE SEASONS. AT 34 YEARS,
324 DAYS HE WAS ALSO THE OLDEST PLAYER TO EVER HIT 50.

50,51

" To be the first player to do it three consecutive years, you go back through the thousands of power hitters who played this game and nobody has ever done it. And I can sit here and say I'm the first ... I'm pretty proud of it."

MARK McGWIRE

Thursday August 20, 1998

McGWIRE 50	Inning	1	Opponent	New York Mets
	Outs	2	Stadium	Shea Stadium
	Count	3-2	Pitcher	Rick Reed
	RBI	1	Distance	385 feet

McGWIRE 51	Inning	7	Opponent	New York Mets
	Outs	0	Stadium	Shea Stadium
	Count	2-1	Pitcher	Willie Blair
	RBI	1	Distance	369 feet

HOME RUN NO. 52 AT
477 FEET THIS WAS THE
LONGEST HOMER EVER
HIT AT PITTSBURGH.
IT WAS ALSO ANOTHER
LANDMARK AS
McGWIRE SETS THE
MAJOR LEAGUE RECORD
FOR THE MOST HOME
RUNS IN CONSECUTIVE
SEASONS—162 IN
THREE YEARS.

Friday August 21, 1998

SOSA 49				
	Inning	5	Opponent	San Francisco Giants
	Outs	1	Stadium	Wrigley Field
	Count	3-2	Pitcher	Orel Hershiser
	RBI	2	Distance	430 feet

Saturday August 22, 1998

McGWIRE 52				
	Inning	1	Opponent	Pittsburgh Pirates
	Outs	2	Stadium	Three Rivers Stadium
	Count	0-2	Pitcher	Francisco Cordova
	RBI	1	Distance	477 feet

53

" I know it's tough. Everybody in baseball knows it's tough. I'm just going to give it my best shot."

MARK McGWIRE

IT'S OUTTA HERE!
FANS CHEER AS THE BALL
CLEARS THE FENCE WHEN
McGWIRE SLAMS NO. 53.

78

" Somebody gets into September with 50, they have a shot down the stretch to either tie, break or get close to the record."

MARK McGWIRE

> " I'm not keeping track, but the record is there for someone to break."

SAMMY SOSA

> " I'm not thinking about that. But I'm not going to lie to you—I'm having a good time."

SAMMY SOSA

SOSA SLAMS HIS 50TH HOME RUN OF THE SEASON IN A GAME WITH THE HOUSTON ASTROS IN CHICAGO. IT WAS THE FIRST TIME HE HAD REACHED THE 50 MARK IN HIS CAREER.

Sunday August 23, 1998

McGWIRE 53				
Inning	8	Opponent	Pittsburgh Pirates
Outs	2	Stadium	Three Rivers Stadium
Count	2-2	Pitcher	Ricardo Rincon
RBI	1	Distance	393 feet

SOSA 50				
Inning	5	Opponent	Houston Astros
Outs	2	Stadium	Wrigley Field
Count	3-2	Pitcher	Jose Lima
RBI	1	Distance	433 feet

SOSA 51				
Inning	8	Opponent	Houston Astros
Outs	0	Stadium	Wrigley Field
Count	1-0	Pitcher	Jose Lima
RBI	1	Distance	388 feet

BIG MAC IS RESTRAINED
BY THIRD BASE COACH
RENEE LACHEMANN AS
HE ARGUES A CALL WITH
UMPIRE SAM HOLBROOK
SHORTLY BEFORE BEING
EJECTED FROM THE
GAME WITH THE
ATLANTA BRAVES ON
AUGUST 29. HIS HOT-
HEADED ACTIONS DENIED
THE ST. LOUIS SLUGGER
THE CHANCE OF FOUR
MORE AT-BATS.

HOMER NO. 52
SOSA'S FIRST HIT IN FOUR
CAREER AT-BATS AGAINST
CINCINNATI REDS PITCHER
BRETT TOMKO.

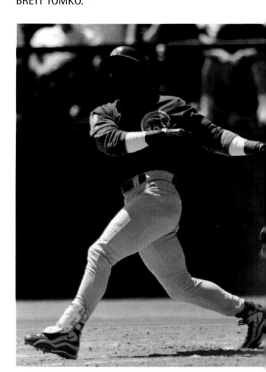

Wednesday August 26, 1998

McGWIRE 54				
	Inning	8	Opponent	Florida Marlins
	Outs	0	Stadium	Busch Stadium
	Count	0-1	Pitcher	Justin Speier
	RBI	2	Distance	509 feet

SOSA 52				
	Inning	3	Opponent	Cincinnati Reds
	Outs	2	Stadium	Cinergy Field
	Count	1-1	Pitcher	Brett Tomko
	RBI	1	Distance	440 feet

SOSA'S HOMER (HIS 53RD OF THE SEASON) WAS HIS 24TH ON THE ROAD AND BROKE THE CUBS CLUB RECORD OF 23 SET BY HACK WILSON IN 1930.

Friday August 28, 1998

SOSA 53				
Inning	1	Opponent	Colorado Rockies
Outs	2	Stadium	Coors Field
Count	1-2	Pitcher	John Thomson
RBI	1	Distance	414 feet

" Yeah, I'm surprised that I'm here right now. I have to say everyone was looking at McGwire and Griffey. But you never know in baseball."

SAMMY SOSA

" I've always swung the same way. The difference is, when I swing and I miss, people say, 'He's swinging for the fences.' But when I swing and make contact, people say, 'That's a nice swing.' But there's no difference. It's the same swing."

SAMMY SOSA

Sunday August 30, 1998

McGWIRE 55				
Inning	7	Opponent	Atlanta Braves
Outs	0	Stadium	Busch Stadium
Count	1-0	Pitcher	Dennis Martinez
RBI	3	Distance	501 feet

SOSA 54				
Inning	1	Opponent	Colorado Rockies
Outs	1	Stadium	Coors Field
Count	1-2	Pitcher	Darryl Kile
RBI	2	Distance	482 feet

Monday August 31, 1998

SOSA 55				
Inning	3	Opponent	Cincinnati Reds
Outs	2	Stadium	Wrigley Field
Count	0-1	Pitcher	Brett Tomko
RBI	2	Distance	364 feet

Tuesday September 1, 1998

McGWIRE 56				
Inning	7	Opponent	Florida Marlins
Outs	0	Stadium	Pro Player Stadium
Count	1-1	Pitcher	Livan Hernandez
RBI	1	Distance	450 feet

McGWIRE 57				
Inning	9	Opponent	Florida Marlins
Outs	1	Stadium	Pro Player Stadium
Count	0-0	Pitcher	Donn Paul
RBI	1	Distance	472 feet

"You never know what can happen, we both have a lot of chances to break it. I'm not thinking about breaking it."

SAMMY SOSA

"This is a great thing that's happening in baseball. We don't know if it will ever happen again."

MARK McGWIRE

" In spring training, it was one of my goals to get 50 homers. Now everything is basically icing on the cake as far as what I can do to strive for ... I surprise myself. It's unbelievable."

MARK McGWIRE

McGWIRE'S TWO HOMERS AGAINST FLORIDA ON SEPTEMBER 1 TOOK BIG MAC TO 57 BREAKING THE NATIONAL LEAGUE RECORD OF 56 SET IN 1930 BY CHICAGO'S HACK WILSON.

" Sammy's a September player, so you have to watch out for him. It's crunch time—time to make history."

MARK McGWIRE

" I know a little about Hack because his picture is next to my locker. I am lucky to be there at the right time. People will now remember two guys, Hack Wilson and myself. And the season is not over yet."

SAMMY SOSA

Wednesday September 2, 1998

McGWIRE 58	Inning	7	Opponent	Florida Marlins
	Outs	2	Stadium	Pro Player Stadium
	Count	2-1	Pitcher	Brian Edmondson
	RBI	2	Distance	497 feet

McGWIRE 59	Inning	8	Opponent	Florida Marlins
	Outs	2	Stadium	Pro Player Stadium
	Count	0-0	Pitcher	Robby Stanifer
	RBI	2	Distance	458 feet

SOSA 56	Inning	6	Opponent	Cincinnati Reds
	Outs	0	Stadium	Wrigley Field
	Count	0-1	Pitcher	Jason Bere
	RBI	1	Distance	370 feet

" Babe Ruth. What can you say—I'm almost speechless. To hear my name alongside his.

I wish I could go back in time and meet him."

MARK McGWIRE

> " I'm being embraced by the public. But also baseball is being embraced."

MARK McGWIRE

HOME RUN NO. 60
CAME IN THE FIRST INNING
OF THE CARDINALS GAME
WITH CINCINNATI AND TIED
McGWIRE WITH BABE RUTH
TO LEAVE HIM ONE SHORT
OF ROGER MARIS' ALL TIME
SINGLE SEASON HOME RUN
RECORD.

> " It's going to be unbelievable, you know. There's going to be a lot of people cheering for Mark McGwire and me. And, hey, we'll see how it goes."

SAMMY SOSA

Friday September 4, 1998

SOSA 57	Inning	1	Opponent	Pittsburgh Pirates
	Outs	2	Stadium	Three Rivers Stadium
	Count	2-0	Pitcher	Jason Schmidt
	RBI	1	Distance	400 feet

Saturday September 5, 1998

McGWIRE 60	Inning	1	Opponent	Cincinnati Reds
	Outs	1	Stadium	Busch Stadium
	Count	2-0	Pitcher	Dennis Reyes
	RBI	2	Distance	381 feet

SOSA 58	Inning	6	Opponent	Pittsburgh Pirates
	Outs	0	Stadium	Three Rivers Stadium
	Count	3-1	Pitcher	Sean Lawrence
	RBI	1	Distance	405 feet

6 1

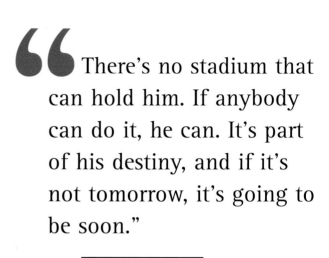

"There's no stadium that can hold him. If anybody can do it, he can. It's part of his destiny, and if it's not tomorrow, it's going to be soon."

CARDINALS RON GANT

"I've been thinking about the record since I reached the 50 plateau. But you think about it and then you let it go because you can't waste many brain cells on hours thinking about it."

MARK McGWIRE

Monday September 7, 1998

McGWIRE 61	Inning	1	Opponent	Chicago Cubs
	Outs	2	Stadium	Busch Stadium
	Count	1-1	Pitcher	Mike Morgan
	RBI	1	Distance	430 feet

MARK McGWIRE TIES ROGER MARIS' MAJOR LEAGUE RECORD WITH HOME RUN NO. 61 IN THE FIRST INNING OF THE CARDINALS CLASH WITH THE CUBS.

MARK McGWIRE SALUTES IN THE DIRECTION OF THE LATE
ROGER MARIS' FAMILY WHO WERE THERE TO WATCH THE ST. LOUIS SLUGGER
EQUAL THE ALL TIME RECORD.

Tuesday September 8, 1998

McGWIRE 62	Inning	4	Opponent	Chicago Cubs
	Outs	2	Stadium	Busch Stadium
	Count	0-0	Pitcher	Steve Trachsel
	RBI	1	Distance	341 feet

THE MOMENT AMERICA HAS WAITED FOR AS McGWIRE KNOCKS THE BALL OVER THE FENCE TO BREAK THE MARIS RECORD AND TO REWRITE THE HISTORY BOOKS. IT WAS ALSO HIS SHORTEST HOME RUN OF THE SEASON.

" I touched Roger's bat
and held it to my heart.
My bat will lie next to his
(in the Hall of Fame). I'm
damn proud of that."

MARK McGWIRE

" What a perfect way to end
the home stand, by hitting 62
for the city of St. Louis and all
the fans. I truly wanted to do
it here and I did.
Thank you St. Louis."

MARK McGWIRE

" The whole country has
been involved in this, I think,
since after the All-Star break.
If people say its bringing the
country together, I'm happy to
bring the country together."

MARK McGWIRE

> " I tell you what, I was so shocked because I didn't think the ball had enough to get out. It's an absolutely incredible feeling. I can honestly say I did it."

MARK McGWIRE

AN EMOTIONAL MOMENT FOR FATHER AND SON, SHARED BY THE WHOLE OF AMERICA. "I HOPE MY SON ONE DAY GROWS UP AND BECOMES A BASEBALL PLAYER AND BREAKS IT," SAID McGWIRE

HOME RUN RIVAL SAMMY SOSA WAS ONE OF THE FIRST TO CONGRATULATE BIG MAC AFTER HE SLAMMED HOMER NO. 62 OF THE SEASON TO BREAK THE RECORD.

> " I sort of missed one big thing—to touch first base. I hope I didn't act foolish, but this is history."

MARK McGWIRE

66 I don't think he (Roger Maris) wanted his record to be broken ... I think he would be happy for Mark and proud for his accomplishments. He would have been proud of Mark as a player, but I think more so as a person."

ROGER MARIS JR.

66 I think it puts baseball back on the map as a sport. It's America's pastime and just look at everyone coming out to the ballpark ... it has been an exciting year."

MARK McGWIRE

SOSA HITS HOMER NO. 59
OFF MILWAUKEE LEFT-
HANDER BILL PULSIPHER
TO END A DROUGHT OF
23 AT-BATS WITHOUT A
HOME RUN.

Friday September 11, 1998

SOSA 59	Inning	5	Opponent	Milwaukee Brewers
	Outs	1	Stadium	Wrigley Field
	Count	0-1	Pitcher	Bill Pulsipher
	RBI	1	Distance	433 feet

Saturday September 12, 1998

SOSA 60	Inning	7	Opponent	Milwaukee Brewers
	Outs	1	Stadium	Wrigley Field
	Count	3-2	Pitcher	Valerio De Los Santos
	RBI	3	Distance	390 feet

THE TRADEMARK HOP AS SOSA BECOMES THE FOURTH MEMBER OF THE 60-HOMER CLUB
WITH A THREE RUN SHOT IN THE SEVENTH INNING THAT LANDED OUTSIDE THE CUBS BALLPARK
AND BOUNCED THROUGH THE FRONT DOOR OF A HOUSE.

"I can't do it every day. They're not going to give me much to hit right now. They're pitching me real well. If I get there, fine. If I don't ... I'm not even thinking about passing McGwire. The season will be over September 27. Mark will go home and I will go to the play-offs."

SAMMY SOSA

SOSA SLUGS A 480-FOOT, TWO RUN HOMER
OFF BRONSWELL PATRICK IN THE FIFTH
INNING TO TIE ROGER MARIS' 61 MARK.

Sunday September 13, 1998

SOSA 61	Inning	5	Opponent	Milwaukee Brewers
	Outs	0	Stadium	Wrigley Field
	Count	0-1	Pitcher	Bronswell Patrick
	RBI	2	Distance	480 feet

SOSA 62	Inning	9	Opponent	Milwaukee Brewers
	Outs	1	Stadium	Wrigley Field
	Count	2-1	Pitcher	Eric Plunk
	RBI	1	Distance	480 feet

" It's unbelievable. It was something that even I can't believe I was doing. It can happen to two people, Mark and I."

SAMMY SOSA

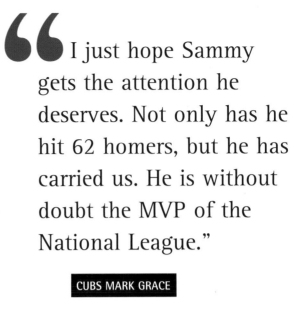

" I just hope Sammy gets the attention he deserves. Not only has he hit 62 homers, but he has carried us. He is without doubt the MVP of the National League."

" At first I thought 61 was something special. The 61 was something that reminded me of Mark. He hit 61 and 62 against us. Then I got 62. It was something unbelievable. I couldn't believe what I was doing. I couldn't believe what was happening."

" Mark, you know I love you. It's been unbelievable. I wish you could be here with me today. I know you are watching me and I know you have the same feeling for me as I have for you in my heart."

HOME RUN NO. 62 WITH ONE OUT IN THE NINTH AND WITH THE CUBS TRAILING 10–8, SOSA TOOK A 2-1 PITCH FROM ERIC PLUNK AND HIT IT OVER THE LEFT-CENTER-FIELD WALL.

"He's been doing it for a year and two months, people cheering, 'C'mon Mark, we want you to hit one.' Boom! He hits one. How does he do it? I have no idea, except that he's remarkable."

CARDINALS MANAGER TONY LA RUSSA

Tuesday September 15, 1998

McGWIRE **63**	Inning	9	Opponent	Pittsburgh Pirates
	Outs	1	Stadium	Busch Stadium
	Count	1-0	Pitcher	Jason Christiansen
	RBI	1	Distance	385 feet

BIG MAC RETAKES THE LEAD IN THE HOME RUN DERBY WITH HOMER NO. 63—AND ENDS A SIX GAME HOME RUN DROUGHT.

" I said to myself I've got to go up there and do it because the New York Mets keep winning every day. The game was on the line and I wanted to go out there and come through for my team. That win tonight means a lot for us."

SAMMY SOSA

Wednesday September 16, 1998

SOSA 63					
	Inning	8	Opponent	San Diego Padres	
	Outs	2	Stadium	Qualcomm Stadium	
	Count	1-0	Pitcher	Brian Boehringer	
	RBI	4	Distance	434 feet	

HOME RUN NO. 63
THE GAME IS TIED WITH THE SAN DIEGO PADRES. TWO OUTS AND THE BASES ARE LOADED. THE CUBS NEED A WIN TO STAY AHEAD IN THE WILD CARD RACE. SOSA NEEDS A HOMER TO CATCH MARK McGWIRE. SOSA STEPPED INTO THE BOX AND LAUNCHED HIS THIRD GRAND SLAM OF THE SEASON.

FOR THE THIRD TIME
IN TEN DAYS, McGWIRE
SETS A NEW STANDARD
FOR HOME RUNS AS HE
SLAMS NO. 64 AGAINST
THE MILWAUKEE
BREWERS.

64

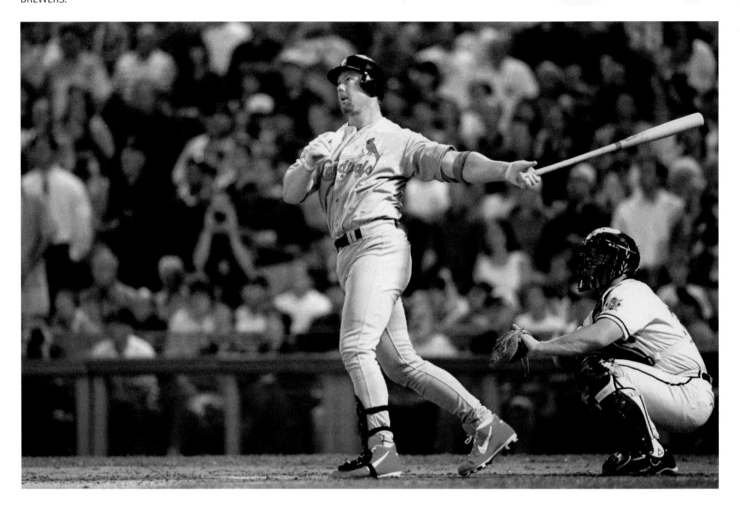

" What he and I have been doing is fantastic. What we've done nobody in the game has done for 37 years.

I'm pretty happy with the way things have been going."

MARK McGWIRE

Friday September 18, 1998

McGWIRE 64				
Inning	4	Opponent	Milwaukee Brewers
Outs	0	Stadium	County Stadium
Count	3-1	Pitcher	Rafael Roque
RBI	2	Distance	410 feet

Sunday September 20, 1998

McGWIRE 65				
Inning	1	Opponent	Milwaukee Brewers
Outs	1	Stadium	County Stadium
Count	2-1	Pitcher	Scott Karl
RBI	2	Distance	420 feet

"You're not supposed to hit 65 homers. We know how important Matthew is to him, but you can't just hit 65 homers because your son asks you to. But here we are with six games left and he has 65. It's unbelievable. 65!"

CARDINALS CATCHER TOM LAMPKIN

McGWIRE MATCHES THE 65 HOMER PREDICTION SET BY HIS SON MATTHEW IN SPRING TRAINING. IT WAS HIS 32ND HOME RUN ON THE ROAD OF THE SEASON.

SOSA SWATS HIS 65TH HOMER OF THE SEASON DURING THE CUBS 8-7 DEFEAT TO THE BREWERS IN MILWAUKEE TO TIE McGWIRE YET AGAIN IN THE GREAT HOME RUN CHASE.

> " I didn't think he hit the ball that hard. The ball just kept going."

BREWERS PITCHER RAFAEL ROQUE

Wednesday September 23, 1998

SOSA 64	Inning	5	Opponent	Milwaukee Brewers
	Outs	1	Stadium	County Stadium
	Count	1-0	Pitcher	Rafael Roque
	RBI	1	Distance	330 feet

SOSA 65	Inning	6	Opponent	Milwaukee Brewers
	Outs	2	Stadium	County Stadium
	Count	2-2	Pitcher	Rodney Henderson
	RBI	1	Distance	410 feet

SOSA WATCHES HOME RUN NO. 64
LEAVE THE PARK AGAINST MILWAUKEE.

"It hurts me to say this because I've pulled for my man as hard as I can, but I think Sosa is the MVP ... he has had a great year, and the Cubs are in the hunt with a week to go in the season. I think that tips it to Sosa."

CARDINALS MANAGER TONY LA RUSSA

"Everyone knows that what happened to me is great. But at the other side I care about winning. I care about the team and the situation right now."

SAMMY SOSA

ANOTHER CURTAIN CALL
FOR SLAMMIN' SAMMY
AFTER HE RIPPED HIS 64TH
HOMER OF THE SEASON.

111

HOME RUN NO. 66
McGWIRE MAKES HIS
POINT TO TIE ONCE MORE
WITH SOSA—THE CHICAGO
SLUGGER'S LEAD LASTED
FOR JUST 45 MINUTES.

66 What he (Sosa) and I have done, whoever's on top, nobody should be disappointed. How can you walk away disappointed if you walk away one below. You can't. It's impossible."

MARK MCGWIRE

Friday September 25, 1998

SOSA 66	Inning	4	Opponent	Houston Astros
	Outs	0	Stadium	The Astrodome
	Count	0-1	Pitcher	Jose Lima
	RBI	1	Distance	420 feet

McGWIRE 66	Inning	5	Opponent	Montreal Expos
	Outs	2	Stadium	Busch Stadium
	Count	1-2	Pitcher	Shayne Bennett
	RBI	2	Distance	380 feet

SOSA CONNECTS WITH
HOMER NO. 66 TO TAKE THE
LEAD IN THE HOME RUN
DERBY FOR THE SECOND
TIME. SOSA ENDED THE
GAME WITH 157 RBIs—THE
FOURTH HIGHEST TOTAL IN
NATIONAL LEAGUE HISTORY.

" As far as I'm concerned, Mark McGwire's home run chase is the most important thing the next two days. It's like heresy for me to say it, but he deserves everything we've got behind him and he's going to get every little bit we do."

CARDINALS MANAGER TONY LA RUSSA

" These guys are amazing. To watch them with all the pressure that's on them, to hit a home run every time. It's really something."

HOUSTON CLOSER BILLY WAGNER

> **"** The worst thing you can do is stop being amazed because you start taking it all for granted."

CARDINALS MANAGER TONY LA RUSSA

McGWIRE RIPS HOME RUN
NO. 68 TO COMPLETE HIS
NINTH MULTI-HOMER GAME
OF THE SEASON AND THE
52ND OF HIS CAREER.

114

ANOTHER CURTAIN CALL FOR THE ST. LOUIS
SLUGGER AFTER HOMER NO. 67.

" It's going to be a relief. I can stop using my mind and stop grinding. I've been grinding since day one. It's not the physical grind; it's the mental grind that's the toughest thing. I've never used my mind anymore than this year ... Sosa and I are the only ones who know what it's like to go through what we've gone through. It's amazing."

MARK McGWIRE

Saturday September 26, 1998

McGWIRE 67				
	Inning	4	Opponent	Montreal Expos
	Outs	1	Stadium	Busch Stadium
	Count	0-0	Pitcher	Dustin Hermanson
	RBI	1	Distance	400 feet

McGWIRE 68				
	Inning	7	Opponent	Montreal Expos
	Outs	2	Stadium	Busch Stadium
	Count	1-1	Pitcher	Kirk Bullinger
	RBI	2	Distance	440 feet

"I think it will
stand for a while.
I know how gruelling
it is to do what I
have done this year.

Will it be broken
some day? It could be.

Will I be alive?
Possibly.

But if I'm not playing
I'll definitely be there."

"This is a season
I will never forget, and
I hope everybody in
baseball never forgets."

Sunday September 27, 1998

McGWIRE 69	Inning	3	Opponent	Montreal Expos
	Outs	2	Stadium	Busch Stadium
	Count	1-1	Pitcher	Mike Thurman
	RBI	1	Distance	380 feet

McGWIRE 70	Inning	7	Opponent	Montreal Expos
	Outs	2	Stadium	Busch Stadium
	Count	0-0	Pitcher	Carl Pavano
	RBI	3	Distance	360 feet

BIG MAC
ACKNOWLEDGES THE
CROWD AFTER
SWATTING THE 69TH
HOMER OF HIS
RECORD-BREAKING
SEASON.

"To say the least I'm amazed. Hitting 70, I've never thought about it or dreamt about it.

When I got to 62 early in September, everybody said, 'Shoot for 70.' I'm speechless, really.

I can't believe I did it. Can you? It blows me away. Then when I came into the club-house after I came out of the game, they already had a 70 homers hat made ...

Obviously it's a huge number. I think the magnitude of this won't sink in for a while.

It's unheard of for somebody to hit 70 home runs.

I'm in awe of myself."

MARK McGWIRE

AT THE END OF THE SEASON BIG MAC HAD DRAWN HIS NATIONAL LEAGUE RECORD WITH HIS 162ND WALK, TYING TED WILLIAMS FOR THE SECOND HIGHEST TOTAL IN MAJOR LEAGUE HISTORY—BEHIND BABE RUTH (170).

> "I'm real happy for him because, hey, he's the man. I'm not thinking about home runs. I have to sacrifice myself for the team."

SAMMY SOSA

> "I don't know if I want to break my own record. I think I would rather leave it as it is. I hope I don't sound too stupid. I wish I had three or four months to think about it."

MARK McGWIRE

THE KING OF HOME RUNS
HIS 70 HOME RUNS OF 1998 TOTALLED 29,588 FEET, NEARLY 400 FEET HIGHER THAN THE PEAK OF MOUNT EVEREST—5.6 MILES OF HOME RUN POWER.

> "It has been a tremendous ride because of Sammy ... We're just two guys who really enjoy playing the game ... I'm really proud of the things I've done this year with Sammy Sosa."

MARK McGWIRE

Babe Ruth's 60 Home Run Season

#	Game	Date	Pitcher, Club	H/A	Inn.	RBI
1	4	Apr 15	Howard Ehmke, Phil.	H	11	1
2	11	Apr 23	Rube Walberg, Phil.	A	1	1
3	12	Apr 24	Sloppy Thurston, Wash.	A	6	1
4	14	Apr 29	Slim Harriss, Bos.	A	5	1
5	16	May 1	Jack Quinn, Phil.	H	1	2
6	16	May 1	Rube Walberg, Phil.	H	8	1
7	24	May 10	Milt Gaston, St. L.	A	1	3
8	25	May 11	Ernie Nevers, St. L.	A	1	2
9	29	May 17	Rip H. Collins, Det.	A	8	1
10	33	May 22	Benn Karr, Cleve.	A	6	2
11	34	May 23	Sloppy Thurston, Wash.	A	1	1
12	37	May 28	Sloppy Thurston, Wash.	H	7	3
13	39	May 29	Danny MacFayden, Bos.	H	8	1
14	41	May 30	Rube Walberg, Phil.	A	11	1
15	42	May 31	Jack Quinn, Phil.	A	1	2
16	43	May 31	Howard Ehmke, Phil.	A	5	2
17	47	Jun 5	Earl Whitehill, Det.	H	6	1
18	48	Jun 7	Tommy Thomas, Chi.	H	4	1
19	52	Jun 11	Garland Buckeye, Cleve.	H	3	2
20	52	Jun 11	Garland Buckeye, Cleve.	H	5	1
21	53	Jun 12	George Uhle, Cleve.	H	7	1
22	55	Jun 16	Tom Zachary, St. L.	H	1	2
23	60	Jun 22	Hal Wiltse, Bos.	A	5	1
24	60	Jun 22	Hal Wiltse, Bos.	A	7	2
25	70	Jun 30	Slim Harriss, Bos.	H	4	2
26	73	Jul 3	Hod Lisenbee, Wash.	A	1	1
27	78	Jul 8	Don Hankins, Det.	A	2	3
28	79	Jul 9	Ken Holloway, Det.	A	1	2
29	79	Jul 9	Ken Holloway, Det.	A	4	3
30	83	Jul 12	Joe Shaute, Cleve.	A	9	2
31	92	Jul 24	Tommy Thomas, Chi.	A	3	1
32	95	Jul 26	Milt Gaston, St. L.	H	1	2
33	95	Jul 26	Milt Gaston, St. L.	H	6	1
34	98	Jul 28	Lefty Stewart, St. L.	H	8	2
35	106	Aug 5	George S. Smith, Det.	H	8	1
36	110	Aug 10	Tom Zachary, Wash.	A	3	3
37	114	Aug 16	Tommy Thomas, Chi.	A	5	1
38	115	Aug 17	Sarge Connally, Chi.	A	11	1
39	118	Aug 20	Jake Miller, Cleve.	A	1	2
40	120	Aug 22	Joe Shaute, Cleve.	A	6	1
41	124	Aug 27	Ernie Nevers, St. L.	A	8	2
42	125	Aug 28	Ernie Wingard, St. L.	A	1	2
43	127	Aug 31	Tony Welzer, Bos.	H	8	1
44	128	Sep 2	Rube Walberg, Phil.	A	1	1
45	132	Sep 6	Tony Welzer, Bos.	A	6	3
46	132	Sep 6	Tony Welzer, Bos.	A	7	2
47	133	Sep 6	Jack Russell, Bos.	A	9	1
48	134	Sep 7	Danny MacFayden, Bos.	A	1	1
49	134	Sep 7	Slim Harriss, Bos.	A	8	2
50	138	Sep 11	Milt Gaston, St. L.	H	4	1
51	139	Sep 13	Willis Hudlin, Cleve.	H	7	2
52	140	Sep 13	Joe Shaute, Cleve.	H	4	1
53	143	Sep 16	Ted Blankenship, Chi.	H	3	1
54	147	Sep 18	Ted Lyons, Chi.	H	5	2
55	148	Sep 21	Sam Gibson, Det.	H	9	1
56	149	Sep 22	Ken Holloway, Det.	H	9	2
57	152	Sep 27	Lefty Grove, Phil.	H	6	4
58	153	Sep 29	Hod Lisenbee, Wash.	H	1	1
59	153	Sep 29	Paul Hopkins, Wash.	H	5	4
60	154	Sep 30	Tom Zachary, Wash.	H	8	2

Roger Maris' 61 Home Run Season

#	Game	Date	Pitcher, Club	H/A	Inn.	RBI
1	11	Apr 26	Paul Foytack, Det.	A	5	1
2	17	May 3	Pedro Ramos, Minn.	A	7	3
3	20	May 6	Eli Grba, L.A.	A	5	1
4	29	May 17	Pete Burnside, Wash.	H	8	2
5	30	May 19	Jim Perry, Cleve.	A	1	2
6	31	May 20	Gary Bell, Cleve.	A	3	1
7	32	May 21	Chuck Estrade, Balt.	H	1	1
8	35	May 24	Gene Conley, Bos.	H	4	2
9	38	May 28	Cal McLish, Chi.	H	2	2
10	40	May 30	Gene Conley, Bos.	A	3	1
11	40	May 30	Mike Fornieles, Bos.	A	8	3
12	41	May 31	Billy Muffett, Bos.	A	3	1
13	43	Jun 2	Cal McLish, Chi.	A	3	3
14	44	Jun 3	Bob Shaw, Chi.	A	8	3
15	45	Jun 4	Russ Kemmerer, Chi.	A	3	1
16	48	Jun 6	Ed Palmquist, Minn.	H	6	3
17	49	Jun 7	Pedro Ramos, Minn.	H	3	3
18	52	Jun 9	Ray Herbert, K.C.	H	7	2
19	55	Jun 11	Eli Grba, L.A.	H	3	1
20	55	Jun 11	Johnny James, L.A.	H	7	1
21	57	Jun 13	Jim Perry, Cleve.	A	6	1
22	58	Jun 14	Gary Bell, Cleve.	A	4	2
23	61	Jun 17	Don Mossi, Det.	A	4	1
24	62	Jun 18	Jerry Casale, Det.	A	8	2
25	63	Jun 19	Jim Archer, K.C.	A	9	1
26	64	Jun 20	Joe Nuxhall, K.C.	A	1	1
27	66	Jun 22	Norm Bass, K.C.	A	2	2
28	74	Jul 1	Dave Sisler, Wash.	H	9	2
29	75	Jul 2	Pete Burnside, Wash.	H	3	3
30	75	Jul 2	Johnny Klippstein, Wash.	H	7	2
31	77	Jul 4	Frank Lary, Det.	H	8	2
32	78	Jul 5	Frank Funk, Cleve.	H	7	1
33	82	Jul 9	Bill Monbouquette, Bos.	H	7	1
34	84	Jul 13	Early Wynn, Chi.	A	1	2
35	86	Jul 15	Ray Herbert, Chi.	A	3	1
36	92	Jul 21	Bill Monbouquette, Bos.	A	1	1
37	95	Jul 25	Frank Baumann, Chi.	H	4	2
38	95	Jul 25	Don Larsen, Chi.	H	8	1
39	96	Jul 25	Russ Kemmerer, Chi.	H	4	1
40	96	Jul 25	Warren Hacker, Chi.	H	6	3
41	106	Aug 4	Camilo Pascual, Minn.	H	1	3
42	114	Aug 11	Pete Burnside, Wash.	A	5	1
43	115	Aug 12	Dick Donovan, Wash.	A	4	1
44	116	Aug 13	Bennie Daniels, Wash.	A	4	1
45	117	Aug 13	Marty Kutyna, Wash.	A	1	2
46	118	Aug 15	Juan Pizarro, Chi.	H	4	1
47	119	Aug 16	Billy Pierce, Chi.	H	1	2
48	119	Aug 16	Billy Pierce, Chi.	H	3	2
49	124	Aug 20	Jim Perry, Cleve.	A	3	2
50	125	Aug 22	Ken McBride, L.A.	A	6	2
51	129	Aug 26	Jerry Walker, K.C.	A	6	1
52	135	Sep 2	Frank Lary, Det.	H	6	1
53	135	Sep 2	Hank Aguirre, Det.	H	8	2
54	140	Sep 6	Tom Cheney, Wash.	H	4	1
55	141	Sep 7	Dick Stigman, Cleve.	H	3	1
56	143	Sep 9	Mudcat Grant, Cleve.	A	7	1
57	151	Sep 16	Frank Lary, Det.	A	3	2
58	152	Sep 17	Terry Fox, Det.	A	12	2
59	155	Sep 20	Milt Pappas, Balt.	A	3	1
60	159	Sep 26	Jack Fisher, Balt.	H	3	1
61	163	Oct 1	Tracy Stallard, Bos.	H	4	1

Mark McGwire

#	Game	Date	Pitcher	Club	H/A	Inn	Outs	Count	RBI	Distance
1	1	March 31	Ramon Martinez	Los Angeles Dodgers	H	5	2	1-0	4	364 feet
2	2	April 2	Frank Lankford	Los Angeles Dodgers	H	12	2	0-1	3	368 feet
3	3	April 3	Mark Langston	San Diego Padres	H	5	0	3-2	2	364 feet
4	4	April 4	Don Wengert	San Diego Padres	H	6	0	2-1	3	419 feet
5	13	April 14	Jeff Suppan	Arizona Diamondbacks	H	3	1	1-2	2	424 feet
6	13	April 14	Jeff Suppan	Arizona Diamondbacks	H	5	2	1-1	1	347 feet
7	13	April 14	Barry Manuel	Arizona Diamondbacks	H	8	0	2-0	2	462 feet
8	16	April 17	Matt Whiteside	Philadelphia Phillies	H	4	2	2-2	2	419 feet
9	19	April 21	Trey Moore	Montreal Expos	A	3	2	0-0	2	437 feet
10	23	April 25	Jerry Spradlin	Philadelphia Phillies	A	7	2	1-2	2	419 feet
11	27	April 30	Marc Pisciotta	Chicago Cubs	A	8	1	2-1	2	371 feet
12	28	May 1	Rod Beck	Chicago Cubs	A	9	2	1-2	2	362 feet
13	34	May 8	Rick Reed	New York Mets	A	3	1	0-2	2	358 feet
14	36	May 12	Paul Wagner	Milwaukee Brewers	H	5	0	1-2	3	527 feet
15	38	May 14	Kevin Millwood	Atlanta Braves	H	4	0	1-1	1	381 feet
16	40	May 16	Livan Hernandez	Florida Marlins	H	4	0	1-0	1	545 feet
17	42	May 18	Jesus Sanchez	Florida Marlins	H	4	0	2-0	1	478 feet
18	43	May 19	Tyler Green	Philadelphia Phillies	A	3	1	2-0	2	440 feet
19	43	May 19	Tyler Green	Philadelphia Phillies	A	5	0	0-2	2	471 feet
20	43	May 19	Wayne Gomes	Philadelphia Phillies	A	8	0	0-0	2	451 feet
21	46	May 22	Mark Gardner	San Francisco Giants	H	6	1	1-1	2	425 feet
22	47	May 23	Rich Rodriguez	San Francisco Giants	H	4	1	1-0	1	366 feet
23	47	May 23	John Johnstone	San Francisco Giants	H	5	1	2-2	3	477 feet
24	48	May 24	Robb Nen	San Francisco Giants	H	12	2	2-2	2	397 feet
25	49	May 25	John Thomson	Colorado Rockies	H	1	2	2-2	1	433 feet
26	52	May 29	Dan Miceli	San Diego Padres	A	9	1	0-1	2	388 feet
27	53	May 30	Andy Ashby	San Diego Padres	A	1	2	0-1	1	423 feet
28	59	June 5	Orel Hershiser	San Francisco Giants	H	1	1	1-2	2	409 feet
29	62	June 8	Jason Bere	Chicago White Sox	A	4	0	0-0	2	356 feet
30	64	June 10	Jim Parque	Chicago White Sox	A	3	1	1-0	3	409 feet
31	65	June 12	Andy Benes	Arizona Diamondbacks	A	3	1	1-0	4	438 feet
32	69	June 17	Jose Lima	Houston Astros	A	3	2	1-2	1	347 feet
33	70	June 18	Shane Reynolds	Houston Astros	A	5	0	1-1	1	449 feet
34	76	June 24	Jaret Wright	Cleveland Indians	A	4	1	1-1	1	433 feet
35	77	June 25	Dave Burba	Cleveland Indians	A	1	2	2-2	1	461 feet

#	Game	Date	Pitcher	Club	H/A	Inn	Outs	Count	RBI	Distance
36	79	June 27	Mike Trombley	Minnesota Twins	A	7	2	2-2	2	431 feet
37	81	June 30	Glendon Rusch	Kansas City Royals	H	7	0	0-1	1	472 feet
38	89	July 11	Billy Wagner	Houston Astros	H	11	1	0-2	2	485 feet
39	90	July 12	Sean Bergman	Houston Astros	H	1	2	0-0	1	405 feet
40	90	July 12	Scott Elarton	Houston Astros	H	7	0	2-1	1	415 feet
41	95	July 17	Brian Bohanon	Los Angeles Dodgers	H	1	2	0-0	1	511 feet
42	95	July 17	Antonio Osuna	Los Angeles Dodgers	H	8	1	1-0	1	425 feet
43	98	July 20	Brian Boehringer	San Diego Padres	A	5	0	2-1	2	458 feet
44	104	July 26	John Thomson	Colorado Rockies	A	4	2	0-0	1	452 feet
45	105	July 28	Mike Myers	Milwaukee Brewers	H	8	1	2-2	1	408 feet
46	115	August 8	Mark Clark	Chicago Cubs	H	4	0	2-1	1	374 feet
47	118	August 11	Bobby Jones	New York Mets	H	4	0	1-0	1	464 feet
48	124	August 19	Matt Karchner	Chicago Cubs	A	8	1	3-1	1	430 feet
49	124	August 19	Terry Mulholland	Chicago Cubs	A	10	1	2-0	1	402 feet
50	125	August 20	Rick Reed	New York Mets	A	1	2	3-2	1	385 feet
51	126	August 20	Willie Blair	New York Mets	A	7	0	2-1	1	369 feet
52	129	August 22	Francisco Cordova	Pittsburgh Pirates	A	1	2	0-2	1	477 feet
53	130	August 23	Ricardo Rincon	Pittsburgh Pirates	A	8	2	2-2	1	393 feet
54	132	August 26	Justin Speier	Florida Marlins	H	8	0	0-1	2	509 feet
55	136	August 30	Dennis Martinez	Atlanta Braves	H	7	0	1-0	3	501 feet
56	138	September 1	Livan Hernandez	Florida Marlins	A	7	0	1-1	1	450 feet
57	138	September 1	Donn Pall	Florida Marlins	A	9	1	0-0	1	472 feet
58	139	September 2	Brian Edmondson	Florida Marlins	A	7	2	2-1	2	497 feet
59	139	September 2	Robby Stanifer	Florida Marlins	A	8	2	0-0	2	458 feet
60	141	September 5	Dennis Reyes	Cincinnati Reds	H	1	1	2-0	2	381 feet
61	143	September 7	Mike Morgan	Chicago Cubs	H	1	2	1-1	1	430 feet
62	144	September 8	Steve Trachsel	Chicago Cubs	H	4	2	0-0	1	341 feet
63	151	September 15	Jason Christiansen	Pittsburgh Pirates	H	9	1	1-0	1	385 feet
64	155	September 18	Rafael Roque	Milwaukee Brewers	A	4	0	3-1	2	410 feet
65	157	September 20	Scott Karl	Milwaukee Brewers	A	1	1	2-1	2	420 feet
66	161	September 25	Shayne Bennett	Montreal Expos	H	5	2	1-2	2	380 feet
67	162	September 26	Dustin Hermanson	Montreal Expos	H	4	1	0-0	1	400 feet
68	162	September 26	Kirk Bullinger	Montreal Expos	H	7	2	1-1	2	440 feet
69	163	September 27	Mike Thurman	Montreal Expos	H	3	2	1-1	1	380 feet
70	163	September 27	Carl Pavano	Montreal Expos	H	7	2	0-0	3	360 feet

Sammy Sosa

#	Game	Date	Pitcher	Club	H/A	Inn	Outs	Count	RBI	Distance
1	5	April 4	Marc Valdes	Montreal Expos	H	3	2	2-1	1	371 feet
2	11	April 11	Anthony Telford	Montreal Expos	A	7	1	1-2	1	350 feet
3	14	April 15	Dennis Cook	New York Mets	A	8	2	3-2	1	430 feet
4	21	April 23	Dan Miceli	San Diego Padres	H	9	0	0-1	1	420 feet
5	22	April 24	Ismael Valdes	Los Angeles Dodgers	A	1	2	3-1	1	430 feet
6	25	April 27	Joey Hamilton	San Diego Padres	A	1	1	0-1	2	434 feet
7	30	May 3	Cliff Politte	St. Louis Cardinals	H	1	2	2-1	1	370 feet
8	42	May 16	Scott Sullivan	Cincinnati Reds	A	3	1	2-1	3	420 feet
9	47	May 22	Greg Maddux	Atlanta Braves	A	1	2	2-2	1	440 feet
10	50	May 25	Kevin Millwood	Atlanta Braves	A	4	0	2-2	1	410 feet
11	50	May 25	Mike Cather	Atlanta Braves	A	8	2	0-1	3	420 feet
12	51	May 27	Darrin Winston	Philadelphia Phillies	H	8	0	1-2	1	460 feet
13	51	May 27	Wayne Gomes	Philadelphia Phillies	H	9	2	0-0	2	400 feet
14	56	June 1	Ryan Dempster	Florida Marlins	H	1	1	1-0	2	430 feet
15	56	June 1	Oscar Henriquez	Florida Marlins	H	8	2	1-0	3	410 feet
16	58	June 3	Livan Hernandez	Florida Marlins	H	5	0	1-0	2	370 feet
17	59	June 5	Jim Parque	Chicago White Sox	H	5	0	1-2	2	370 feet
18	60	June 6	Carlos Castillo	Chicago White Sox	H	7	2	2-2	1	410 feet
19	61	June 7	James Baldwin	Chicago White Sox	H	5	1	3-2	3	380 feet
20	62	June 8	LaTroy Hawkins	Minnesota Twins	A	3	1	0-2	1	340 feet
21	66	June 13	Mark Portugal	Philadelphia Phillies	A	6	0	0-1	2	350 feet
22	68	June 15	Cal Eldred	Milwaukee Brewers	H	1	2	1-0	1	420 feet
23	68	June 15	Cal Eldred	Milwaukee Brewers	H	3	1	2-1	1	410 feet
24	68	June 15	Cal Eldred	Milwaukee Brewers	H	7	2	2-1	1	415 feet
25	70	June 17	Bronswell Patrick	Milwaukee Brewers	H	4	0	2-2	1	430 feet
26	72	June 19	Carlton Loewer	Philadelphia Phillies	H	1	2	2-2	1	380 feet
27	72	June 19	Carlton Loewer	Philadelphia Phillies	H	5	1	1-0	2	380 feet
28	73	June 20	Matt Beech	Philadelphia Phillies	H	3	2	3-2	2	366 feet
29	73	June 20	Toby Borland	Philadelphia Phillies	H	6	1	2-0	3	500 feet
30	74	June 21	Tyler Green	Philadelphia Phillies	H	4	2	2-2	1	380 feet
31	77	June 24	Seth Greisinger	Detroit Tigers	A	1	1	0-2	1	390 feet
32	78	June 25	Brian Moehler	Detroit Tigers	A	7	0	1-0	1	400 feet
33	82	June 30	Alan Embree	Arizona Diamondbacks	H	8	1	3-2	1	364 feet
34	88	July 9	Jeff Juden	Milwaukee Brewers	A	2	2	0-2	2	432 feet
35	89	July 10	Scott Karl	Milwaukee Brewers	A	2	0	1-0	1	438 feet

#	Game	Date	Pitcher	Club	H/A	Inn	Outs	Count	RBI	Distance
36	95	July 17	Kirt Ojala	Florida Marlins	A	6	2	2-1	2	440 feet
37	100	July 22	Miguel Batista	Montreal Expos	H	8	2	1-0	3	365 feet
38	105	July 26	Rick Reed	New York Mets	H	6	1	2-2	2	420 feet
39	106	July 27	Willie Blair	Arizona Diamondbacks	A	6	2	1-1	2	350 feet
40	106	July 27	Alan Embree	Arizona Diamondbacks	A	8	0	0-0	4	420 feet
41	107	July 28	Bob Wolcott	Arizona Diamondbacks	A	5	1	3-1	4	400 feet
42	110	July 31	Jamey Wright	Colorado Rockies	H	1	2	3-2	1	380 feet
43	114	August 5	Andy Benes	Arizona Diamondbacks	H	3	2	3-2	2	380 feet
44	117	August 8	Rich Croushore	St. Louis Cardinals	A	9	0	1-0	2	400 feet
45	119	August 10	Russ Ortiz	San Francisco Giants	A	5	2	3-1	1	370 feet
46	119	August 10	Chris Brock	San Francisco Giants	A	7	2	2-1	1	480 feet
47	124	August 16	Sean Bergman	Houston Astros	A	4	1	0-1	1	360 feet
48	126	August 19	Kent Bottenfield	St. Louis Cardinals	H	5	2	0-0	2	368 feet
49	128	August 21	Orel Hershiser	San Francisco Giants	H	5	1	3-2	2	430 feet
50	130	August 23	Jose Lima	Houston Astros	H	5	2	3-2	1	433 feet
51	130	August 23	Jose Lima	Houston Astros	H	8	0	1-0	1	388 feet
52	133	August 26	Brett Tomko	Cincinnati Reds	A	3	2	1-1	1	440 feet
53	135	August 28	John Thomson	Colorado Rockies	A	1	2	1-2	1	414 feet
54	137	August 30	Darryl Kile	Colorado Rockies	A	1	1	1-2	2	482 feet
55	138	August 31	Brett Tomko	Cincinnati Reds	H	3	2	0-1	2	364 feet
56	138	September 2	Jason Bere	Cincinnati Reds	H	6	0	0-1	1	370 feet
57	139	September 4	Jason Schmidt	Pittsburgh Pirates	A	1	2	2-0	1	400 feet
58	142	September 5	Sean Lawrence	Pittsburgh Pirates	A	6	0	3-1	1	405 feet
59	148	September 11	Bill Pulsipher	Milwaukee Brewers	H	5	1	0-1	1	433 feet
60	149	September 12	Valerio De Los Santos	Milwaukee Brewers	H	7	1	3-2	3	390 feet
61	150	September 13	Bronswell Patrick	Milwaukee Brewers	H	5	0	0-1	2	480 feet
62	150	September 13	Eric Plunk	Milwaukee Brewers	H	9	1	2-1	1	480 feet
63	153	September 16	Brian Boehringer	San Diego Padres	A	8	2	1-0	4	434 feet
64	158	September 23	Rafael Roque	Milwaukee Brewers	A	5	1	1-0	1	330 feet
65	158	September 23	Rodney Henderson	Milwaukee Brewers	A	6	2	2-2	1	410 feet
66	159	September 25	Jose Lima	Houston Astros	A	4	0	0-1	1	420 feet

Acknowledgments

This project was conceived, co-ordinated and designed by Russell Porter, Design Director at Carlton Books, London, during a frantic three weeks in September, 1998, with the encouragement of a fellow baseball fan, Thom Duffy, an American journalist who spent five years in London. It has been produced by individuals passionate about baseball. All have a deep respect for Mark McGwire and Sammy Sosa, whose words and actions, both on and off the field, have inspired this book's creation.

In appreciation for all their efforts, the publishers would like to thank the following:

NEW YORK:
GEORGE VECSEY—for his carefully chosen words at a particularly busy time and at very short notice.

THOM DUFFY—for his networking, his enthusiasm and efforts in contributing to all aspects of the book.

ALLAN LANG and KEITH ALLEN-JONES—for their commitment and belief in the book.

CHICAGO:
BILL ADEE—for his help and encouragement.

ST. LOUIS:
BRIAN ILES—for being there.

ATLANTA:
RANDY FREEDMAN—for his updates and for being at the end of the phone.

LONDON:
FIONA MARSH—for all her support in difficult times.

DAVID ELLIS—a native of New York now living in London, for his words and meticulous attention to detail.

TODD MACKLIN—and everyone else at Channel 5's MLB programme for a great show.

Carlton Books:
CHRIS HAWKES *(project editor)*—special thanks for his absolute dedication, his commitment from day one and his support at desperate moments over the last three weeks.

LORNA AINGER, JUSTIN DOWNING *(picture research)* and MARK LLOYD *(jacket design)*—for always coming up with the goods.

JOHN MAYNARD and SARAH SCHUMAN *(production)*—for all their efforts in getting the back end right.

JOSHUA PORTER and LIAM DUFFY
Two three-year-old kids, Liam in New York and Joshua in London, who will grow up no doubt hearing of this amazing story from their fathers and the book they produced. As the boys grow older, this home run story will become a focus of everything good in sport—to recognise excellence, to achieve the impossible, and to play with respect. In Mark McGwire and Sammy Sosa, these young fans, and millions like them, could have no better sporting heros and role models.

Picture Credits

The publishers would like to thank the following sources for their kind permission to reproduce the pictures in this book:

Allsport USA 40-1, 84, 88-9/Brian Bahr 64-5, 66, Tim Brokema 100, Jonathan Daniel 8-9, 49, 51b, 101tr,tl, 102, 103t,b, 104-5, Stephen Dunn 50, Kathleen Economou 110, 111b, Jed Jacobsohn 1, 2-3, 5br, 91, 92, 94, 95, 96, Vincent Laforet 7, 24-5, 53, 54, 59, 69, 99, 120-1, Rick Stewart 76, Matthew Stockman 5bl, 12-3, 56-7, 72-3, 106, 108, 109t,b, 111t

AP 5t, 31, 67/Leon Algee 23, 55, 113t, Al Behrman 80b, H.Darr Beiser 86t, Mary Butkus 20, 21, 32-3, 48b, 52, 58, Jay Crihfield 38, Gary Dineen 51t, John Dunn 74, Eric Draper 83t, 93, James A Finley 30t,b, 98b, 114t, 124, 115, 116, Mike Fisher 44, 126, Tom Gannam 29, John Gaps III 68t,b, 80t, 114c, 118t, Michael S Green 62, 71, 79, Elsa Hasch 97, 98c, Osamu Honda 28b, Kent Horner 107, Lenny Ignelzi 26, Fred Jewell 42, 48tr,tl, Tim Johnson 113bl, Beth A. Keiser 70, 101b, Rusty Kennedy 27, Mark Lennihan 28t, Ken Levine 39, 61, Jim Mone 37, David J.Philip 113br, Frank Polich 34, 36, 63, Denis Poroy 35, Gene J. Puskar 78, Ed Reinke 18, 98t, 117, 118b, 119t,b, Amy Sancetta 83b, 86b, 90, 112, 114b, Richard Sheinwald 19, 46, 47, David Zalubowski 81

Corbis/UPI 16, 17, 123

Hulton Getty 14, 15, 122

Every effort has been made to acknowledge correctly and contact the source and/copyright holder of each picture, and Carlton Books Limited apologises for any unintentional errors or omissions which will be corrected in future editions of this book.

Special thanks to Jane Gowman at AP, Paul Ashman, Rob Harborne, Mark Webbon at Allsport UK Ltd.